MY FAMILY'S STUMBLING STONES

Over 400 years of family stories, scandals, secrets and tall tales

by

ANNE L. ECKSTEIN

Published by Brolga Publishing Pty Ltd
ABN 46 063 962 443
PO Box 452
Torquay 3228 VIC
Australia

email: markzocchi@brolgapublishing.com.au

ISBN: 978 176 368 0142

Printed in Australia
Cover design by Luke Harris, WorkingType Studio
Typeset by WorkingType Studio

This book is dedicated to
Tom, Evie and Wolfie Eckstein:

Once you know where you have come from,
you can work out where you are going.

Preface

Stolpersteine (stumbling stones)[1] have turned up on streets and footpaths all over Europe – over 90,000 of them. They remember victims of Nazi persecution; mostly Jews but also homosexuals, Jehovah's Witnesses, Slavic and Roma people, communists and many others, who opposed the regime. From an idea by German artist Günther Demnig, small concrete cubes are set into the ground and each has a 10cm square bronze plaque on it, which is inscribed with a name, a birth date, what happened to them, and when and where they died. They are intended to make us 'stumble' out of our complacency and make sure that their names and lives will never be forgotten. The Talmud says, "A person is only forgotten when his or her name is forgotten."

For most of us, what we know about our own families, our 'living memory', is limited to about three generations. We know about our parents and our children; perhaps our grandparents; our aunts and uncles, our nephews, nieces and cousins, but very little else. It seems to me that just as the 'stumbling stones' help us to remember lives tragically lost, we need something similar to 'stumbling stones' to help us remember our long lost family members, how they lived their lives and what this can tell us about ourselves. However, I don't want to suggest that long lost family members are in any way the same as people remembered by the actual 'stumbling stones'.

---

1 See Stolpersteine and Günther Demnig's websites for more information, including https://www.stolpersteine.eu/

It has taken almost 15 years to unravel and build my family tree from the early 1600s to the 21st century. Most of the people I never knew, yet they lived lives and had families, raised children, achieved things or not as the case may be. There are also many things I have learnt from some of my ancestors, and some others that I really wish I had not. But you cannot just choose to claim those bits of history you like and ignore the hard and unpleasant things. Truth-telling is important even if it is sometimes ugly.

The stories in this book make up my past and have contributed to who I've become. There is much that I still don't know: people I have yet to find and information that is missing. Many questions remain to be answered and perhaps never will be. However, the strands are coming together and many elements can be traced from things and people that have long since faded into the mists of time.

We all need to know where we have come from and where we have been; how else can we know where we are going?

Anne L Eckstein

Contents

Acknowledgements

No one can undertake a project of this size and complexity without help from a lot other people. I am indebted to my good friend Carolyn Hirsh for her review and editing of this book. I also thank Sigi and Heidi Messner for their thoughts on the content and direction of the book.

I would like to thank my various Eckstein and Trefz cousins, and in particular my cousin Sigi (Siegfried) Messner, my aunt Lotte (Charlotte Emma) Trefz nee Thomas (1920-2018) and my mother's cousin Hartmann Trefz (1928-1914) for generously sharing their stories, photographs and documents. In particular, Sigi Messner provided input right from the outset. Gisela Trefz Meyer and Lorraine Aylett Messner also helped to fill in some of the gaps. In Germany, Jörg Kübler from Neuweiler provided much information on the Aichele family, as did Margarete Nestel nee Hummel, now deceased, from Reutlingen, who helped me join the dots in my grandmother Aichele's family. Also my German Eckstein cousins: Ilse Wilde nee Weinsdörfer, Richard Eckstein and his son Helmut, as well as Richard's sister Gertrud Eckstein Huber and her husband Michael, all helped facilitate my access to family documents and memories.

The Eckstein's from Stöckach, Roβtal, Christenmühle and surrounding areas provided three family trees as well as access to memories, photographs and paintings of various Eckstein ancestors. Their acceptance of me turning up on their doorsteps out of the blue when they didn't even know I existed is especially admirable. Johann Völkl, mayor of Roβtal in 2012 and also an Eckstein descendant was very welcoming both when I first contacted him be email and when I met him in person. He also gave me a family tree and some books on Roβtal, which complemented and expanded the many other documents I was given by more immediate family members.

I am very grateful to Brunnhilde Zörner nee Trefz for her comprehensive history of the Fürstenhof: *600 Jahre Fürstenhof 1393–1993, Geschichte und Geschichten*, published in 1993 for an insight into the Trefz family origins and the early history of this village and those who lived there. This book was generously given to me by her daughter, Jutta Zörner, in 2012.

Hans-Peter Rosenberger from Kichheim am Neckar, a family historian in his own right, facilitated my access to the church records and the town's archives, where I was able to inspect and photograph the original *Inventarium* of some of my Trefz ancestors. He also took me to the Fürstenhof and to the Stegmühle where we were able to gather further documents and memories from more Trefz descendants.

Käthe Greiner from Kirchheim am Neckar is my third cousin and she generously provided access to a range of letters, photographs and memories of the Trefz ancestors to the times when Johann Jakob Trefz took his second family into the Temple Society at the Kirschenhardthof near Erbstetten.

In addition, the Trefz family at the Stegmühle very generously provided me with a family tree and histories dating back to their origins on the Fürstenhof. One Sunday morning in 2012, Gustav Trefz and his wife Irma nee Müller and their son Bernhard, who are also direct descendants of Jacob Treffz (1645-1693), (and therefore are my 7th and 8th cousins, once removed), generously shared their documents, photographs and information with a 'blow-in' from Australia who turned up unannounced on their doorstep.

Bill Weaver, my third cousin in the United States, descendant from my great-grandfather's younger sister, provided lots of information on the American side of the Trefz familiy.

Also, Andrew Mayer, my 3rd cousin once removed, gave me access to Christina Sophie Trefz' diary from 1870.

The Trefz family connections to the Templers is a story by itself and a number of people need to be thanked for expanding my knowledge and insights. Dr Ejal Jacob Eisler, who knows more about the Templers in Palestine than most Templers themselves do, was able to identify the location of some of my old photographs and shared his depth of knowledge during two Templer trips to Palestine. Peter Lange, Tempelgesellschaft Deutschland historian and Doris Frank, Temple Society of Australia historian provided valuable assistance and insights, especially with historical documents and Templer records. Charlotte Weller Dravenieks nee Asenstorfer, now deceased, was able to give me an insight from a first-hand account of life in Templer Palestine and especially in the Jaffa, Walhalla and Sarona colonies in the 1920s and 1930s.

Jürgen Herrmann from Nürnberg and Friedrich Bürger from Mitwitz helped me sort out my Kunstmann ancestors.

A big thank-you goes to *Ancestory.com* for providing a comprehensive family history website for managing an enormous family tree of almost 40,000 people, and tools for accessing and incorporating records and information on the lives of those ancestors.

Without the considerable help of all of these people (and anyone else I should have included here but have forgotten), this book would not have been possible. Any errors, mistakes or misinterpretations are, of course, entirely my responsibility.

Anne L Eckstein
January 2024

Introduction

I wouldn't be the first child, in a fit of anger, to have wondered how they could possibly have sprung from one or other of their parents' loins or even wished that they were adopted rather than admit to some part of their parentage. So delving into my family history is not about confirming or denying parentage, although inevitably you find things you wish you hadn't.

Some time ago I embarked on a journey about my family and where they came from. ('Journey'; how I hate that word! Everyone is on a journey these days and so the word has become a meaningless epithet for everything from spiritual self-discovery to a new work skill to a trip to Bali!) And yet it was a journey; of discovery and growth, and at times of surprise and even shock.

It started when I received an email from a member of the Templer[2] community in Germany asking about the Trefz family. My mother's maiden name was Trefz. While I knew my extended family in Australia: aunts and uncles, cousins and the names of my grandparents, I knew precious little about the background of the family except that my great-grandfather's name was Christoph and that he had lived in 19th century Palestine with other German Templers in semi-rural communities known as colonies.

In following up the email, I was sent a family tree with the names of Trefz ancestors that I had never heard of before. As

---

2 The Temple Society, nothing to do with the Knights Templar, developed from the Friends of Jerusalem, a German pietist movement founded by Christoph Hoffmann (1815-1885) in the mid-19th century. See also the Section on *The Friends of Jerusalem (Templers)* and the Bibliography for further references.

it was a quiet day at work and I had managed to get onto the Ancestry.com website, I decided to search for one of the unknown names from the family tree: Johann Jakob Trefz, supposedly my great-great-grandfather. To my surprise, not only did a personal record pop up but it led to a family tree. That family tree was full of people I knew; my aunts and uncles, my mother's cousins, my grandfather and his brother Wilhelm. This was too much to be a coincidence; besides, I don't believe in coincidences! I made contact with the owner of the tree and found my third cousin, Bill Weaver, in the United States, who is descended from my great-grandfather's younger sister, Sophia Christina Mayer née Trefz.

Since then, I have found many more family members, both living and long since gone. I have traced the families of my four grandparents: Trefz, Aichele, Eckstein and Kunstmann from Germany to the USA; from Palestine to Australia; and to other places around the world. It has been far more like a quest for knowledge; like doing a jigsaw puzzle where lots of the pieces are either blank or missing and where you have to make some of the pieces as well as put them in the right places.

I have also learned about the lives of my ancestors; their big stories and big adventures as well as the little and ordinary ones; and the important contributions of their lives and their day-to-day struggles. I have looked into old pictures of ancestors I never knew; looked into their eyes and faces to see past lives and reflections down the generations to me and my contemporaries. As William McInnes[3] wrote in his Foreword *to Little Picture/Little Story*, the catalogue for one of his wife's photographic exhibitions:

---

3 McInnes, William, 2011, from the Foreword In: *Little Picture / Little Story*, catalogue for Sarah Watt's last photographic exhibition, quoted In: *When I'm gone...*, The Age newspaper, 22 October 2011

"...What struck me wasn't only the beauty of the images but the idea behind them, that the whole picture if you like, is made up from countless other little pictures. And that each of these little pictures is a world unto itself. Life's biggest questions, and any chance of an answer, can be posed on the smallest or most domestic of canvases."

And so it is with people's lives and with their stories....

I hope and trust that these stories will not only be interesting and perhaps sometimes entertaining, but that they may also provide some insights into lives lived well, and not so well lived; lived in the wake of the greater historical events of their times and the ordinary world of daily life, work and family. They attempt to honour both those that came before and enrich the understanding of those that come after. Because, if you don't know where you have come from, how can you move forward into the future?

Australia's First Nations people have a strong and enduring relationship with their history, their land and their ancestors which hold lessons for us all:

The past is not lost. It is all around us; ever present and shaping our future. It lives within us...[4]

In order to respect the privacy of those who had no say about how their family's ancestors are portrayed in this book, I have not included identifying details of those younger than my own generation and have rarely even mentioned their names. They know who they are and I know who they are! They are included on my full Eckstein Trefz Family Tree on

4 Rachel Perkins (daughter of Charles Perkins). Boyer Lecture 1, 2019

Ancestry.com, but are excluded from public view while they are still living.

I have made every attempt to make sure that what follows is correct and have, wherever possible, footnoted the sources of the information that has been included. However, I am fully to blame for any mistakes or incorrect interpretations of the original information.

Anne L Eckstein
January 2024

1. Beginnings of the Trefz Family

The first reference to the family name Trefz in the Backnang area comes in the year 1393[5] in the *"Lagerbuch: Zinsen und Gülten auf dem Land und der Stadt Backnang"* (Asset Register: Interest and payments in the countryside and the city of Backnang), where a widow Trefz, who had a house next to the bath-house near the top bridge in Unterweissach has to pay three shillings in interest. Unfortunately, I cannot connect any of my ancestors to this widow Trefz but clearly the name goes back a long way in this part of Germany.

I have followed my Trefz ancestors back over 400 years and about 10 generations to British Mandate and Ottoman Palestine, to Kirchheim am Neckar in Württemberg and before that, to the Fürstenhof near Großaspach. (Großaspach is near Backnang to the north of Stuttgart in Württemberg, Germany.) There are many stories; large and small, of significant achievements as well as ordinary life in those 400 plus years. There are also many gaps in the larger family history and many questions, which still go unanswered. There is much further work left for future generations to do.

The early history of many families in Germany is a bit sketchy. Germany has no regular census collections as in the United States, the United Kingdom and Australia. Family records of births, deaths and marriages, at a time when many ordinary people were illiterate, were kept by the local Minister or Priest in the parish

5 Zörner, Brunnhilde: 600 Jahre Fürstenhof 1393–1993, *Geschichte und Geschichten*, p. 12

records (*Kirchenbücher*). The Thirty Years War (1618-1648) was a watershed which saw many churches and monasteries sacked and many of the earlier records destroyed. Records from before this time are rare survivors of a period of brutal religious civil war, not unlike the English Civil War of 1642 to 1651. Further wars on European soil, including two World Wars: 1914-1918 and 1939-1945 also contributed to the loss of important documents, as well as many personal items, photographs and artefacts. I never cease to be surprised that so many records still remain.

Three Farmers buy the Fürstenhof

My Trefz family comes from Groβaspach near Backnang in Württemberg, Germany. Although it must go back a lot further, I begin my story in 1675[6], when three farmers, Michael Läpple, Albrecht Traub and my 7th great-grandfather, **Jakob Treffz (1645-1693)**, bought a small sheep farming estate called the Fürstenhof near Groβaspach together with the surrounding fields, pastures and the woodlands. It was bought for 2000 Gulden or fl. (guilders) from the local duke[7], who was in need of some urgent cash and ongoing regular income.

2000 fl. would have been an enormous sum for ordinary working people to pay in 1675. In fact, they paid a deposit of 200 Gulden and were expected to make yearly payments of 100 Gulden beginning in 1676, which made the deal a bit

---

6 ibid. p. 22-26 and Treffz, Hermann: Die Ähre, Mitteilungsblatt der Familie Trefz, Gerlingen bei Stuttgart, hrg. Familienarchiv Trefz, date unknown

7 Guilder comes from Dutch and was the form of currency in southern Germany in the 17th century. It was originally a gold coin and the abbreviation is "fl." (= "*florin*"), which in German is called "*Gulden*". There were also a range of other coins and different denominations used in the various German states at this time. Gulden were abolished in 1873 when the German Mark was introduced, not long after the unification of the German states into one country in 1871.

more manageable. As well, they had to pay annual interest of 32 Gulden and provide an amount of spelt (*Dinkel*) and oats (*Hafer*) to the duke.

The sale also included:

- The farmhouse together with its rotten gable
- The crops still in the fields
- All the farm equipment and chattels, including carts and cow chains
- 8 oxen and steers
- 5 cows
- A third of the 6-month old steers (*Farren*)
- 28 sheep and lambs
- The woodlands with 11 oak trees that the farmers agreed to fell at their own expense.

The Fürstenhof[8] originally belonged to the principality of Württemberg. In 1524, the "*Schaffhoff Fürstenberg*" included a house, a barn, a small garden and a stable and was worth 100 Gulden. Herzog Eberhard III von Württemberg bought the estate in 1666, barely 9 years before it was sold again by his son, Wilhelm Ludwig (1647-1677) to the three farmers. In 1675, the Fürstenhof estate was run down and unproductive, and being used mostly as a princely estate (*Kammergut*), probably used for hunting and for producing food for his lordship's household. The land had been neglected and buildings were also in poor condition, so much so that the gable of the farmhouse was rotten and needed to be replaced. The sheep and lambs were of poor quality. The sale of the Fürstenhof to the three farmers in 1675 allowed the duke to rid himself of a costly, unproductive asset and secure an ongoing income for a number of years. It also

---

8 Zörner, Brunnhilde: *600 Jahre Fürstenhof 1393–1993*, Geschichte und Geschichten, p. 20ff

marked the transfer of the land from the nobility into the hands of ordinary people.

Although times were not always easy, the Fürstenhofers eventually made quite a good living from the estate and progressively turned it into productive farmland [9]. They mostly grew spelt, rye and oats but also some other grains, such as canola (*Raps*), millet (*Hirse*), peas, beans as well as vegetables for their own use. On their pastures, they raised mainly sheep, pigs and some cattle for both milk and meat, but they also had chickens, ducks, geese, oxen and some horses. There was also forestry from a small woodland. While there had been some wine-growing in the past, it was never a major industry in the area. Farming sustained the Fürstenhofers better than most through the difficult times of the 18th and 19th centuries and even into the 20th century. In 1816-1817[10] there was widespread crop failure in Germany (and the rest of Europe) when the Indonesian volcano Krakatoa erupted and the dust caused large-scale climate change. The unusually high rainfall in those years led to the seeds rotting in the ground. As a result, the animals got sick from the poor pastures, so there was also a shortage of milk and meat as well as little flour and other grains.

It was in the same year that the three farmers bought the Fürstenhof that Jakob Treffz married **Maria Weidlin[11] (1654-1709)** also from Groβaspach and they went on to have nine children. My 8th great grandfather, and Jakob's father, was Hanns Treffz from Groβaspach. He and his wife Anna were presumably born sometime before around 1620, but that is all that is known about them. There was another Treffz named

9 ibid. p.43-44

10 ibid. P.33

11 German women's family names often added the suffix 'in', while men added 'en' in the 17th an 18th centuries.

Jakob[12] and his wife Katharina living in Groβaspach at the same time as Hanns Treffz. His descendants also lived and worked on the Fürstenhof. It seems likely they were related, perhaps even brothers. It may be possible to trace them further back and connect them through the church and civilian records in Groβaspach, Rietenau and Backnang but that is a job for another time and another generation.

Jakob Treffz and Maria Weidlin had nine children together:

- Magaretha (1676-unknown)
- Daniel (1668-1761)
- Anna Maria (1679-1680)
- Gabriel (1681-1681)
- Anna Christina (1682-1759)
- Maria (1684- unknown))
- **Johann (Hans) Ulrich Treffz (1686-1756)**, my 6th great grandfather,
- Andreas (1688-1755); and
- Johann (Hans) Jakob (1693-1730)

The Trefz, Läpple and Traub families lived on the Fürstenhof for many generations and had many childrenIn 2012, there were two women still living on the Fürstenhof, who were born with the maiden name Trefz, and there are probably many more Trefz descendants.

A dead calf and shot in the calf

Hanns Michael Treffz (1672-1740) from Groβaspach married Anna Maria Läpple (1675-1740) from the Fürstenhof. Hanns Michael's father was Hans Jakob Treffz (1647-1719) from Groβaspach, who was a descendant of the Jacob Treffz from

12 Treffz, Hermann: Die Ähre, Mitteilungsblatt der Familie Trefz, Gerlingen bei Stuttgart, hrg. Familienarchiv Trefz, date unknown

Groβaspach who lived there at the same time as Hanns Treffz, the father of the Jakob Treffz, who bought the Fürstenhof. This Hans Jakob may have been a cousin to my Jakob Treffz and here is his story.

In the years after the three farmers took over the Fürstenhof,

The Trefz barn at the Fürstenhof in 2012.

there was regular strife with the farmers from surrounding villages over grazing rights to the Fürstenhof pastures. This came about because the 1675 contract of sale for the Fürstenhof estate did not specify the right to graze the land, either for the new Fürstenhof owners, or for the surrounding villagers who had grazed these pastures for many years when they belonged to the nobility.

In 1703[13], there was a major clash between the Fürstenhofers and the farmers from Kirchberg and Rielingshausen. After threatening words and some pushing and shoving, Hanns Michael Treffz shot and killed a calf belonging to the

13 Zörner, Brunnhilde: 600 Jahre Fürstenhof 1393–1993, Geschichte und Geschichten, p.54ff.

Kirchbergers and then shot Phillip Layer, a Kirchberger, through the calf of his leg (*Wade*) with his shotgun, probably a flintlock or a musket (*Flinte*) [14]. Treffz then took off with the Kirchbergers in hot pursuit, but he couldn't be caught. The Fürstenhofers were held responsible by the local authorities, who imposed penalties on the Fürstenhofers, including 15 fl. for the dead calf, 36 fl. for medical costs and pain and suffering for the 'damaged' Philipp Layer as well as a fine of 56 fl. The squabbles with nearby villages over grazing rights continued for at least the next 100 years.

A Trefz buys the Stegmühle

Jakob Treffz' oldest son Daniel (1678-1761) remained on the Fürstenhof as did many of his descendants. About a hundred years later in 1815, Daniel's great-grandson, also Daniel (1794-1866) left the Fürstenhof and bought the nearby Stegmühle

The Stegmühle in 2012

14 'Shotgun' doesn't quite describe this weapon, which was probably more like a flintlock or a musket.

about 3 km away. The mill has been owned by his descendants ever since (as at 2012), although it is no longer a working mill. They are also direct descendants of Jacob Treffz (1645-1693) and therefore are my 7th and 8th cousins, once removed.

The mill, which still stands today, was built in 1799 and last ground wheat into flour in 1961. It is still being restored to its former glory by its 5th generation owners: Gustav Trefz and his wife Irma nee Müller and their son Bernhard. Bernhard is a historian by profession and has an extensive family tree and family archive, parts of which he shared with me in 2012.

2. The Trefz in Kirchheim am Neckar[15]

Hannss Ulrich Treffz marries a Kirchheimer

The move to Kirchheim am Neckar comes with **Hannss Ulrich Treffz[16] (1686-1756)**, my 6th great grandfather, who moved there to marry a local girl. Hannss Ulrich was born at the Fürstenhof as the seventh of nine children and the third son of Jakob Treffz. As a middle son, he was unlikely to inherit at the Fürstenhof. He was a tailor and a farmer[17] by trade. Other records[18] say he was a *Weingärtner* (wine grower) and Kirchheim am Neckar has, of course, long been known as a wine-growing region.

On 9 September 1710 at the age of 24, he married **Anna Barbara Hartmann (1687-1745)** from Kirchheim. His *Inventarium*, a legal document outlining the assets of both partners upon entering into a marriage, is still in the city archives. In 2012, I was in the Archives in Kirchheim am Neckar, holding the original 300 year old document in my hands, and able to read a part of my ancestor's life story. The *Inventarium* runs to only 8 pages and lists only a small number of possessions, including clothes, tools and household goods, such as linen.

---

15 There are two families named Trefz in Kirchheim am Neckar dating back to the early 18th century but they are not related to one another. My family comes from Hannss Ulrich Treffz (1686-1756).

16 There was almost no spelling standardisation at this time and his family name is also spelled Treffz, Trefts, Treffts, Treffz and Trefz, depending on the document and / or the transcriber

17 Kirchheim am Neckar Kirchenbuch 2, P. 214

18 ibid, P 456

Anna Barbara died in 1745 and less than a year later Hannss Ulrich remarried a widow: Rosina Catharina Schneider nee Grimm. We know nothing about her or their relationship except that Hans Ulrich lived another 10 years before he too died.

Hannss Ulrich and Anna Barbara had five children (that we know of):

- Johann Jakob (1711-unknown)
- Anna Barbara (1713-unknown), who later married Johann Georg Allgayer,
- **Johann Wendel Treffz (1717-unknown)**, my 5th great grandfather,
- Johann Andreas (1724-unknown); and
- Johann Georg (1727-1730).

Nothing more is known about the lives of their children.

Winemaker Johann Wendel Trefz

My 5th great grandfather, **Johann Wendel Trefz (1717-unknown)**, was born 8 Aug 1717 in Kirchheim am Neckar. He was a *Weingärtner* (wine grower) by trade and, unlike his father, is referred to in the church records as a *Bürger,* a citizen of the city of Kirchheim am Neckar[19]. This shows that the Trefz family was now an accepted part of this community, which gave him a certain position and carried with it obligations, such as paying taxes.

On 2 October 1742, he married **Maria Barbara Riekher**, the daughter of another Kirchheimer wine grower. They had 10 children together:

- Johann Jacob (1745-1745), died at seven months;
- Johann Wendel (1746-1826), aged 80 years;

19 Kirchheim am Neckar Kirchenbuch 1, P. 433

- Maria Margareta (1749-1828), aged 79 years;
- Maria Barbara (1751- unknown);
- **Johann Christian Trefz (1753-1805)**, aged 52 years and my 4th great grandfather;
- Johann Michael (1756-1832), aged 76 years;
- Johannes (1758-1767), aged 9 years;
- Johann Georg (1760-1760), died at one week;
- Anna Katarina (1762-unknown); and
- Christina Magdalena[20] (1766-unknown).

We know very little about the other children, apart from my ancestor, Johann Christian, and Johann Michael. Most of Johann Michael's children remained in and round the Württemberg area of Germany. However, one of his grandsons emigrated to New Brunswick in Canada, where the name Trefz was anglicised to Trifts. Some of this family later moved to Ohio and Massachusetts in the United States.

Citizen Johann Christian Trefz

Johann Christian Trefz (1753-1805), my 4th great grandfather, was also a *Bürger* (citizen) of Kirchheim and a *Weber* (weaver) by trade. He married **Maria Magdalena Baüchlin** on 14 November 1780 in Winzerhausen[21]. They had 10 children but half of them died as infants:

- **Georg Jacob Trefz (1781-1838)**, aged 57 years and my 3rd great grandfather;
- Maria Margarete (1783-1783, died at five days;
- Johann Christian (1784- unknown);
- Johannes (1787- unknown);

20 Christina Magdalena does not appear in Kirchenbuch 2, P. 456 but was found through Ancestry.com

21 Kirchheim am Neckar Kirchenbuch 1, P. 433

- Johann Wendel (1788-1789), died at 10 months;
- Johann Georg (1790-1791?), died at seven months;
- Friederich (1792-1816), aged 24 years;
- Twins: Andreas and Gottlieb (1794-1794), died at five days and two weeks respectively); and
- Johann Wendel (1801-1801), died at six months.

Councillor Georg Jakob Trefz

My 3rd great grandfather was **Georg Jakob Trefz (1781-1838)**[22] and lived in Kirchheim am Neckar. He married **Catharina Maria Barbara Rosenberger (1784-1885)** on 3 June 1804. They had only two children. Johann Jakob Trefz, my great-great-grandfather, was born on the 9th of August 1806. His only sibling, Margaretha Barbara Trefz, was born in 1805 and died at the age of three and a half years in 1808. Church records show entries for two other children in 1814 and 1815 crossed out, who both appear to have died at birth. As a result and rather unusually for a time of very large families, my second great-grandfather grew up as an only child.

Like his father before him, Georg Jacob was also a *Bürger* and *Weber* in Kirchheim am Neckar. The church records show a later addition indicating that he became *Gemeinderath* (a town or parish councillor)[23]. Not only was he a citizen, he was a piller of his community. He was also a man of some means, having bought a substantial farmhouse at Mühlgasse Number 23[24] in 1825[25]. The River Neckar once flowed where the railway bridge on the right of the photo on page 17 now stands.

---

22 Kirchheim am Neckar Kirchenbuch 1, P. 433b

23 ibid

24 Photograph of 23 Mühlgasse, Kircheim am Neckar by Anne Eckstein in May 2012

25 Gebäude-Güterbuch der Gemeinde Kirchheim am Neckar, P. 151

Georg Jacob Trefz' house at Mühlgasse 23 in 2012

Johann Jakob Trefz marries the girl next door

Johann Jakob Trefz (1806-1881) was my great-great-grandfather. Rather unusually for the time, he was an only son and grew up as an only child. His older sister died when he was just two years old. This was confirmed by his granddaughter, Emma Sophia Weaver Bird nee Mayer (1885-1985) in notes she wrote about her family in the 1980s[26]. Johann Jakob grew up in and later inherited his father's farmhouse in Kirchheim am Neckar at Mühlgasse Number 23. Next door, towards the river, lived the Kleinmanns, who owned and ran a flour mill. The mill was washed away in the great flood of the river Neckar of 1824[27]. The flood must have destroyed the Kleinmann's entire livelihood.

26 Emma Weaver Bird nee Mayer's notes on her family per Hartmann Trefz, circa early 1980s

27 Personal communication, Hans-Peter Rosenberger and Käthe Greiner in May 2012

On the 22 September 1831 at the age of 25, Johann Jakob Trefz married the girl next door, Esther Louisa Kleinmann (1811-1846). He had eight children with Esther before she died in 1846. She died of pneumonia at the age of 35, about a month after the birth of her last child. The baby also died about a week after the mother's death from failure to thrive since birth. It seems likely that they both died as a result of complications from the birth. Those eight children include[28]:

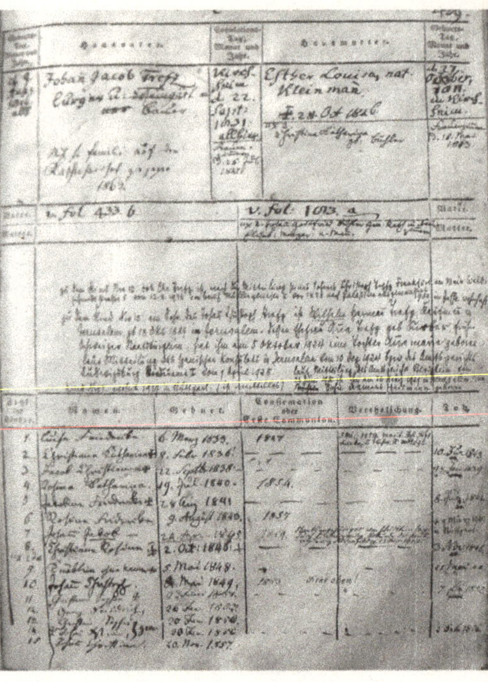

Kirchheim am Neckar, protestant church, *Kirchenbuch* extract (see p216 for larger version)

- Luise Friederike (6 May 1833-30 Jun 1890), aged 57 years;
- Christiane Katharine (8 Feb 1836-10 Jun 1843), aged 7 years;
- Jakob Christian (22 Sep 1838-18 Jan 1839; aged four months)
- Rosina Katharina (19 Jul 1840-10 May 1919), aged almost 69 years;
- Jakobine Friederike (28 Aug 1841-8 Jun 1842), aged nine months;

28 Photograph of Johann Jakob Trefz' entry in the Kirchhheim am Neckar parish register P. 439 by Anne Eckstein in May 2012

- Rosine Friederike (Rike) (9 Aug 1843-22 Oct 1902), aged 59 years;
- Johann Jakob (24 Apr 1845-9 Mar 1929[29]), aged 79 years; and
- Christiane Rosine (2 Oct-3 Nov 1846), aged 1 month.

Within a year of Esther's death, Johann Jakob married for a second time. This was very common in the days when many women and babies did not survive childbirth. Even if they did, they often succumbed to fevers and infections shortly afterwards. It was also before there were effective treatments for serious and even quite ordinary infections. Babies also died from lack of breast milk if the mother died early. The husbands were then left with a tribe of young children and no spouse; so they soon remarried, if only to have someone to care for the children. This usually led to more children with the second or even third wife.

This was the case with Johann Jakob Trefz. In 1847, aged 42 years, and only 9 months after Esther's death, he married Christina Katharina Bühler. Christina was aged 34 years when she married him and there is no evidence that she was married before, or that she brought children from a previous relationship into the marriage.

Christina bore Johann Jakob Trefz another seven children, including a set of twins[30]:

- Unnamed baby boy (5 May-11 May 1848), aged six days;
- **Johann Christoph**, my great-grandfather, **(8 May 1849-21 Apr 1895)**, aged 46 years;
- Christine Sophia (2 Jun 1851-7 Feb 1852), aged eight months;

29 While the church record shows he died in 1929, there is information that he actually died in 1924.

30 Ibid Photograph of Johann Jakob Trefz' parish register entry

- Georg Friedrich (26 Jan 1853-4 Feb 1919), aged 66 years;
- Johann Christian, twin to Christine Sophie, (20 Jan 1856-2 Feb 1856), aged two weeks;
- Christine Sophie, twin to Johann Christian (20 Jan 1856-9 Sep 1906), aged almost 51 years; and
- Johann Christian (20 Nov 1857-27 May 1912), aged 55 years.

Johann Jakob Trefz was by all accounts a wealthy man. His granddaughter, Emma Weaver Bird née Mayer remembers her mother talking about a summer house in Kirchheim am Neckar, investments in Stuttgart, a farm in Hochdorf and a flour mill among his assets[31]. In 1863 he sold up all his property, including the house at Mühlgasse Number 23, to join a pietist religious group, who called themselves the Friends of Jerusalem (later the Templers). They had set up a Christian community at the Kirschenhardthof, not far from Backnang. The Kirschenhardthof was a mixed farming property where the community could gather, grow food and sustain itself. The Templers planned to emigrate to the Holy Land to live the Kingdom of God on earth and await the imminent second coming of Jesus Christ in Jerusalem. The Templers also ran a school for lay preachers at the Kirschenhardthof and conducted Confirmation classes for teenagers in the community.

31 Emma Mayer Weaver's notes on her family per Hartmann Trefz, circa early 1980s

3. The Trefz become Templers

The Trefz family's links to the early Templers comes from Johann **<u>Jakob</u> Trefz (1806–1881)**, who sold up everything he owned in 1863 to move his second wife and family to a Templer farming community. The Kisrchenhardthof estate was bought by the Templers in 1856 as a base and as a precursor for future settlements, first in present day Ukraine and later in the Holy Land.

In 1869[32], Johann Jakob's son and my great-grandfather, **Johann Christoph Trefz, (1849–1895)** emigrated to Palestine aged 20 years and ultimately settled in Jerusalem. This was at the same time as many of the earliest Templers also arrived and the first two colonies at Haifa and Jaffa were established. But, there is no evidence that he travelled with a Templer group[33].

The Templers wanted to live a simple life in a Christian community to create God's Kingdom on earth. Ultimately, three generations of Trefz lived in Palestine and called it home.

In 1863, Johann Jakob Trefz, sold up all his property and settled up with the children from his first marriage, adding a document to his *Inventarium*[34] setting out each of their entitlements from his fortune. The oldest child was already married and as a sizeable amount had already been spent on her wedding, she was to receive nothing more.

---

32 See Johann Christoph's entry in Johann Jakob Trefz' parish register entry

33 Many Templers travelled to the Holy Land in groups called *Wanderzüge* (migrations, literally wandering trains or caravans).

34 Photograph of Addendum to Johann Jakob Trefz' Inventarium, Archive, Kirchheim am Neckar by Anne Eckstein, May 2012

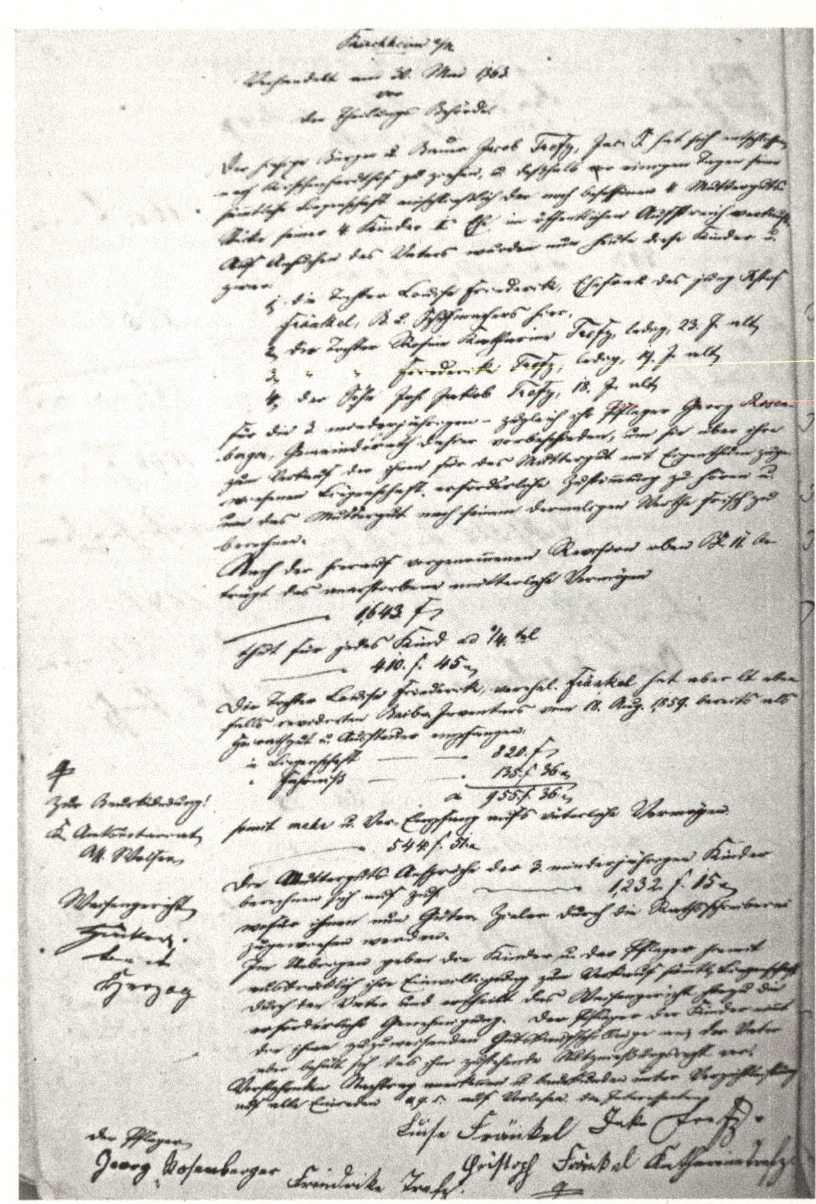

The Addendum to Johann Jakob's *Inventarium* from 1863

The adult children each signed the document, agreeing to the arrangements, while Georg Rosenberger, their guardian (*Pfleger*), signed on behalf of the minor children. Johann Jakob then moved his second family to the Kirschenhardthof, a small farming community near the village of Erbstetten.

The Kirschenhardthof was not only a farming community to sustain the growing Templer flock, but also a base for living the Templer belief in a simple Christian community and for the theological training of lay preachers and missionaries, who would spread Christoph Hoffmann's[35] teachings in the world; including as far away as the United States of America and Russia[36].

The Friends of Jerusalem (Templers)

Because the Templers have played such a big part in the lives of my Trefz ancestors for the last 160 years or so, it is important to understand something of their history and religious beliefs. What motivated them to leave their homes in Germany and give up everything that was familiar to set up largely agricultural settlements, firstly in present day Ukraine[37] and then in the Holy Land? Disillusionment with the State Church of Württemberg as well as some powerful beliefs and faith, a charismatic leader are all part of the story.

---

35 Christoph Hoffmann (1815-1845) was the spiritual founder of the Temple Society (formerly *Jerusalemfreunde* or Friends of Jerusalem) and its religious beliefs.

36 Paul Sauer, *The Holy Land Called: The Story of the Temple Society*, translated by Gunhild Henley, published by The Temple Society Melbourne, 1991, Page 37

37 Templer settlements in southern Russia, in what is now Ukraine, include: Gnadenfeld, Tempelhof and Orbeljanowka, Olgino, Wohldemfürst and Alexanderfeld. For further information, see: *Damals im Kaukasus: Ein Erzählbuch*, published by Tempelgesellschaft Deutschland, Stuttgart, 2001

Why did they stay in the Middle East for so long? Undoubtedly they grew to have a connection to the land even though they would always call Germany home. Why did so many come to settle in Australia? It was not only because some of their family members were interned here during World War 2 and chose to stay on afterwards. It was partly that the creation of the State of Israel in 1948 and the holocaust perpetrated by the Nazi regime meant there could never be a return to the Templer colonies in the Holy Land. It was also because of the similarities between life in Australia and Palestine. I too sensed the connection on my trips to Israel in 2012 and 2016: the climate, the vegetation and the lifestyle all reminded me of my Australian home. I also felt the connections to Jaffa and Israel more strongly than I ever felt them to Augsburg, my father's home in Germany.

Although, in 1969, I was confirmed in the Templer faith, I remember absolutely nothing about my confirmation lessons. Fortunately, **my 2nd great aunt, Christine Sophie Trefz (1856-1906)**[38] from the United States of America, kept detailed notes of her confirmation lessons in 1870[39], which provide useful insights into their early beliefs and why the Templers went to the Holy Land. Her journal contains 17 weekly lessons on the main features of Templer beliefs as well as an overview of the Confirmation service. I have also looked at some Templer histories for an overview of the main historical milestones and key early beliefs.

Christoph Hoffmann's and Templer beliefs evolved over time. The early Templers were millennialists, believing that the second coming of Jesus Christ was imminent and the

38 Photo courtesy of William Frederick Weaver, Connecticut, USA

39 Transcript and translation of Christine Sophie Trefz' diary of 1870 by Anne Eckstein, 2013

gathering of God's people in Jerusalem was central to it. They also believed in living a good and simple Christian life as outlined in the Scriptures and in building communities to create God's Kingdom on Earth.

They had a strong belief in the literal meaning of prophecy, both from the Old Testament and in the Revelations of Saint John in the New Testament. The early Templers also placed great importance on the charismatic gifts of the Holy Spirit. These include: knowledge and wisdom, increased faith, (faith) healing, miracles, prophecy, recognising spirits, and the understanding and interpretation of tongues.

Some of the main points in Christine's journal are:

- Deciding to follow the right path to God
- Wisdom comes from fear of God
- Death and illness come from sin and can only be overcome through belief in God
- A person must strive to become *ein Tempel Gottes* (part of the Kingdom of God)
- Turning to the Kingdom of God and following God's commandments as given by Moses conquers evil/the devil
- The way to God's Kingdom is through the gospels and teachings of Jesus Christ
- Individual conscience is the way for each person to find the Kingdom of God
- Prayer is individual communication with God

Christine Sophie Trefz (1856-1906)

- The charismatic gifts are needed to build a Christian community and God's Kingdom
- Prophecy gives insight into the future and therefore is to be taken literally rather than allegorically
- Confirmation in the church is where a person makes the decision to follow God
- Confirmation is needed for taking Communion and is the start of religious adulthood.

Christine would have been 14 at the time of her Confirmation; she would have already finished school and perhaps even have been working in the home or in the community. (There was a Templer tradition for girls of that age to work for two years with other Templer families for room and board so they learnt how to cook, clean and keep house in preparation for marriage.) Her journal is written in beautiful copperplate handwriting, presumably copied from a chalk board or perhaps dictated.

Communion (*Abendmahl*) is no longer a religious practice among Templers today and neither is infant baptism, while Confirmation still takes place. *Darstellung* (a presentation service to introduce infants into the Templer community) has replaced the sacrament of baptism. Joining the Templer faith requires an informed decision and commitment made by an adult. There are no "rigid dogmas, fixed creeds, sacraments or rituals"[40]. Much weight is placed on individual conscience and in living a good Christian life according to the Scriptures. Contemporary Templer beliefs still centre on seeking the Kingdom of God on earth:

> *"Set your mind on God's Kingdom and His justice before everything else, and all the rest will come to you as well." (Matthew 6:33)*

---

40 The Temple Society: An Overview, TSA, Melbourne, 1986, Page 1.1

Gottlob Christoph Jonathan Hoffmann (1815-1885)

Gottlob Christoph Jonathan Hoffmann (1815-1885) was the spiritual founder of the Temple Society. He grew up in the Korntal Community of Brethren, a pietist community in the State of Württemberg, Germany. He later studied theology, where he was exposed to the religious thinking of the day. At the time there was no separation of church and state in Württemberg and he became progressively more and more disillusioned with the corruption and the economic and social hardships he saw around him, and especially with the State Church's complete failure to address these. Eventually, as his teachings deviated more and more from those of the official church, Hoffmann split from the Württemberg State Protestant Church.

Georg David Hardegg (1812-1879)

Hoffmann teamed up with Georg David Hardegg (1812-1879), who was a more down to earth, practical man. He was a merchant from near Ludwigsburg. As a young man in the 1830s, he took up revolutionary and republican ideas, which eventually landed him in jail. There, he spent a lot of time reading the Bible and other religious writings, including those of Christoph

Hoffmann. He agreed with Hoffman's religious ideas and joined his 'Friends of Jerusalem' community. Hardegg became the worldly leader and managed the day-to-day operations; he took over leadership of the Haifa colony when Hoffmann moved his base to Jaffa.

In 1854, a public meeting organised by Hoffmann, Hardegg, and Hoffmann's brothers-in-law, Christoph Paulus and Louis Höhn, resulted in 439 signatures on a petition, where the undersigned formed the Society for the Gathering of the People of God in Jerusalem. The petition was worded as follows:

> *"We have formed a society with the intention of building communities in the Holy Land which strive to replicate the conditions of the first apostolic community in Jerusalem. The code of law for these communities is the Holy Scripture of the Old and New Testaments. The communities shall be the beginning of a people whose chosen task is the fulfilment of Divine Law under all life conditions so that Jerusalem will become a source of light for Christianity and the whole world."*[41]

In 1856, the Templers bought an agricultural property, the Kirschenharthof near Erbstetten, both to educate lay preachers and as a trial for setting up future colonies in the Holy Land. In 1861, the Templers were formed as an independent religious society with this declaration:

> *"In view of the general disorientation of mankind caused by the fact that none of the existing churches aspires to making man into a temple of God and to establish the sanctum of*

41 Origins of the Temple Society, translation of *Wie es zum Tempel kam* by Peter G Hornung, TSA, Melbourne 2003, Page 16

> *Jerusalem for all nations, we, the undersigned, disassociate ourselves from Babylon, that is to say from the existing churches and sects, and unite to establish the German Temple, to carry out the Law, the Gospel and the Prophecy."*[42]

Templer *Gemeindehaus* at Kirschenhardthof, where community members lived, lay preachers were trained and meetings were held, as it was in 2012.

A fact-finding expedition to the Holy Land in 1858, found the country to be almost uninhabitable for westerners and it was decided to postpone the relocation of the community to Palestine. In 1867, some 'rogue' families moved to Palestine on their own, without support and approval from the Templer leadership. It all ended in tragedy. Haifa became the first successful and official Templer colony in the Holy Land in 1868.

When the first Templers went to Palestine in the mid-19th century it was hardly God's Kingdom on earth; it was more

42 Paul Sauer, *The Holy Land Called: The Story of the Temple Society*, translated by Gunhild Henley, published by The Temple Society Melbourne, 1991, Page 36

like the end of the earth. It was a forsaken outpost of the Ottoman Empire. Although many Christian denominations had churches, orders and missions in Palestine's holy places, life in the towns and cities was basic. Some European religious orders ran clinics and hospitals but they could not deal with more complex cases.

Agricultural technology was primitive even by 19th century European standards. The climate was harsh; the land was arid or swamp-ridden and malaria infested. Tropical diseases, particularly fevers such as malaria, and bilharzia (also known as snail fever), a disease caused by a water-born parasitic worm, were rife. I had an uncle who died of bilharzia as a child of eight years. In fact, the first and unauthorised Templer settlement in Samunieh 1867 at Chnefiss on the western slope of the hills near Nazareth ended in disaster with all of the settlers eventually succumbing to fever and disease.

The first official Templer colonies were established in Haifa 1868 and Jaffa in 1869. In Jaffa, the Templers took over the wooden houses abandoned by the George Adam's settlers from Maine, who had returned to the United States after only 12 months in the Holy Land. These were followed by the agricultural colony of Sarona in 1871, where oranges were mostly grown for export to Germany. The Jerusalem colony, where the future Templer headquarters would be built on the Rephaim plain, just outside the Old City, followed in 1873. Wilhelma, another agricultural settlement, was opened in 1902; Walhalla near the original Jaffa colony in 1903; and Bethlehem Galilee in 1906. Waldheim near Bethlehem was a 'Kirchler'[43] settlement established in 1907.

In 1874, there was a schism in the Templer community. It

---

43 The Kirchlers were the followers of Hardegg who returned to the German protestant church after the schism.

took the Great Schism of 1054 for the eastern (Orthodox) and the western (Roman) Christian churches to go their separate ways, although the roots of this split go back to 800 and the crowning of Charlemagne by Pope Leo III, completely sidelining Byzantine Christianity.

It took western Christianity another 500 years or so and Martin Luther for the Protestants to split from the Roman Catholic Church. It took the Templers just 25 years.

Christoph Hoffmann and Georg David Hardegg had a falling out over Hardegg building himself a rather grand house in Haifa. About a third of the Templers, mostly from Haifa, left with Hardegg and became known as the Kirchlers. Waldheim, near Bethlehem Galilee, became a Kirchler settlement/colony. After Hardegg's death, most of the Kirchlers re-joined the official German protestant church rather than go back to the Templers. Today, Hardegg's grand house in Haifa rather appropriately houses a humble kindergarten.

After Hoffmann moved from Haifa to Jaffa, he based the Templer headquarters there in the former home of Platon Grigorievich, Baron von Ustinow (1840-1918). Baron von Ustinov had a garden with exotic plants and animals, which my mother still remembered from the 1920s and 1930s. The building was also once the Hotel du Parc, which was considered the only place in the colony suitable for hosting Kaiser Wilhelm 2[44] and his party in 1898.

After the establishment of the Jerusalem colony, Hoffmann relocated the Templer head-quarters there and the Templers had achieved their goal of a spiritual home in the Holy Land. At this site in the German Colony on the corner of Beit Lehem Road and Emek

---

44 Kaiser Wilhelm 2 and his wife Auguste Victoria visited the orient and in particular, Palestine in 1898 to dedicate the German Lutheran Church of the Redeemer in Jerusalem. He also visited the Templer colonies of Haifa and Jaffa and held talks with their leaders.

Refa'im Street, a community hall opened in 1883, a secondary school for boys transitioned students into the German education system and an administration building provided leadership for the community until the Templers were displaced by World War 2. The school and administration building have recently become a multi-storey 5-star hotel but the community hall is still being used by the Armenian Christian church for services.

The second wife dies in the poorhouse

Johann Jakob Trefz moved his family into the Templer community at Kirschenhardthof in 1863. Little is known about his and the family's time there. He was 57 when he moved to the mostly farming community. There is evidence of an approved application for a building permit for agricultural buildings, including barns and sheds from March 1864[45]. Several of his children were confirmed in the Templer faith, including Christine Sophie Trefz in 1870, whose diary[46] of detailed notes of her confirmation lessons has survived and is today in the possession of her descendants in the United States of America. It provides an insight into the beliefs of the early Templers, including their literal beliefs in the Scriptures and Prophecy.

On 9 September 1873[47], after almost 10 years at Kirschenhardthof amongst the Templer community, Johann Jakob Trefz was "excluded from the German Temple (Deutschen Tempel) without his family"[48]. There is no record of what he

---

45 Building permit application: Hakius, Georg und Trefz, Jakob vom Kirschenhardthof (Hochberg): Scheunen- und Schuppenanbau, genehmigt am 4.3.1864, Staatsarchiv Ludwigsburg F 210 II Bü 1274

46 Transcript and translation of Christine Sophie Trefz' diary of 1870 by Anne Eckstein, 2013

47 Personal communication from Peter Lange, Templer historian, 2012

48 ibid

Johann Jakob Trefz house in Hochberg in Küferstraße.

did to incur the wrath of the Templers and to warrant this punishment (or conversely what they did to incur **his** wrath!).

Perhaps it was a disagreement about how the community was being run; perhaps the community in Germany was being depleted by steady streams of emigrants to Palestine. It was around this time that the Templers sold the Kirschenhardthof to focus on their settlements/colonies in the Holy Land. As Johann Jakob was 67 years old by this time, travel and resettlement in Palestine were probably not practicable for him. Perhaps he had opposed the decision to sell the Kirschenhardthof.

Some years later, in 1875, he had a large, rather smart, house built in nearby Hochberg at Küferstraße 34-36[49] where, on 8 July 1881, he died, aged 74 years.

Descendants of Johann Jakob's first daughter by his first wife Esther Kleinmann claim[50] that Johann Jakob was so drawn into the Templer vision and beliefs by Christoph

49 Personal communication from Christoph Remmele, Stadtarchivar, Remseck am Neckar, June 2015

50 Personal communication from Käthe Greiner, May 2012

Hoffmann and his followers, that he gave them his entire and substantial fortune. They also claim that as a result, his second wife, Christina Katarina née Bühler (1813-1896), died penniless in the poorhouse.

This is not true. The archivist in Remseck am Neckar has confirmed that she died on 3 September 1896 at the age of 83 years at home, at the substantial house in Hochberg in Küferstraße 34-36[51].

51 Personal communication from Christoph Remmele, Stadtarchivar, Remseck am Neckar, June 2015.

4. Johann Jakob's many children

As was fairly common for the times, almost half of Johann Jakob Trefz senior's 15 children from his two marriages did not survive to adulthood. Four of his eight children with his first wife Esther Kleinmann died as young babies:

- Christiane Katharine at seven years
- Jakob Christian at four months
- Jakobine Friederike at nine months
- Christiane Rosine at one month.

Rosina Katharina Trefz (1840-1910)

Another three of the seven children from his second marriage also died in infancy:

- Unnamed baby boy at 6 days
- Christine Sophia at 8 months
- Johann Christian, twin to Christine Sophie Trefz, at 2 weeks.

Of the remaining eight children, four never married or had children:

- **Rosina Katharina**[52] (19 July 1840 – 10 May 1910) died at aged 69 years, 10 months in Connecticut, USA

52 Photo courtesy of William Frederick Weaver, Connecticut, USA

- **Rosine Friederike (Rike)** (9 August 1843 – 22 October 1902). There is a memory by a descendant of Johann Jakob's eldest daughter, Luise Friederike Fränkel née Trefz of a cousin Rike (*die Rike Bas'*)[53] living not far from Kirchheim. There is also a note[54] dated 28 June 1890, written to Rike by her stepmother (Johann Jakob's second wife), when her sister, Luise Friederike Fränkel lay dying. Rike would have been 47 years old at the time. Rike died 12 years later in 1902 at the age of 59 years in Frauenzimmern.
- **Johann Jakob** Junior (24 April 1845 – 9 March 1924) died penniless and destitute in Germany, aged 79 years. He spent some years living and working with his siblings in Connecticut, USA. It seems he went backwards and forwards between Germany and the USA several times according to the church records in Kirchheim am Neckar, which record gaps in his being there. Trefz descendants in Connecticut still have one of his expired passports
- **Georg Friedrich (Fritz)** (26 January 1853 – 14 February 1919) died in Connecticut, USA aged 66 years. Fritz lived with his half-sister Rosina Katharina in the same house in Connecticut all the time they were in America.

Georg Friedrich Trefz (1853-919)

53 Bas' is dialect for Base, an archaic German term for a female cousin.

54 Note dated 28 June 1890 from Andreas David Rosenberger to his wife's step-grandmother Christine Katharine Trefz née Bühler, who then forwarded it onto her step-daughter Rike (Friederike) in the possession of Käthe Greiner, scanned by Anne Eckstein May 2012

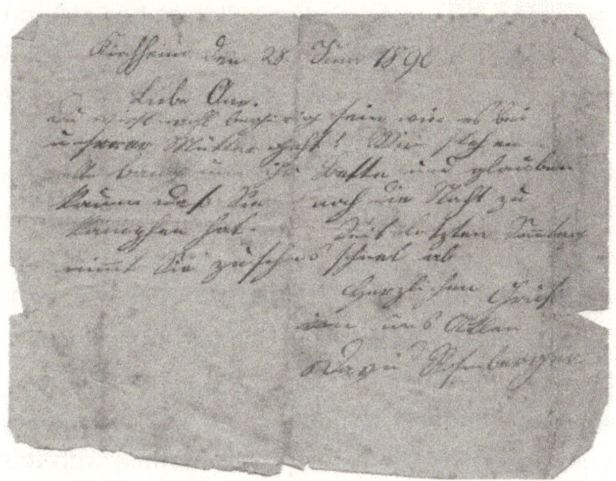

Kirchheim, the 28th June 1890 / Dear Am / Du wirst wohl begierig sein wie es bei unserer Mutter geht! Wir stehen alle bang um ihr Bette und glauben kaum, daβ Sie noch die Nacht zu kämpfen hat. Seit letzten Sonntag nimmt sie zusehens schnel (sic) ab. / Herzlichen Gruβ von uns Allen / David Rosenberger

Liebe Rike so eben wurde ich erschreckt mit dem Brief jezt (sic) was machen wenn du sie nur besuchen känst (sic). Es grüβt dich deine Mutter

Remaining unmarried and/or childless has also been the case in several subsequent generations, although I was not so much aware of it in my immediate family and always felt like the odd one out because of it.

Only four of Johann Jakob TREFZ (senior's) children married and had children. Their descendants now live in Germany, the USA and Australia.

Johann Christian Trefz' (1857-1912) only son, **Willi Oskar Trefz (1892-1917)**, died in 1917 in Flanders from injuries received in the First World War and so ended his line. Johann Jakob senior's descendants from the remaining three children no longer carry the Trefz name. The last male with the family name Trefz, was my mother's first cousin, **Hartmann Trefz (1929–2014)** and the son of **Wilhelm Hermann Trefz (1887–1959)**, who died in his mid-eighties in 2014, single and with no children.

The Trefz who stayed in Kirchheim

There is a descendant of Johann Jakob's eldest daughter (from his first marriage), **Luise Friedrike Trefz (1831-1890)** still living in Kircheim am Neckar today (2024). Luise married a local boy Johann Christoph Fränkel (1832-1912) and three generations of their descendants also lived in Kirchheim. In his 1863 Addendum to his Inventarium, Johann Jakob noted that as Luise had already had a considerable amount spent on her marriage, she should receive nothing more from his estate.

Luise and Christoph Fränkel had a daughter and two sons. Their daughter, **Christine Katherine Fränkel (1860-1935)** married **Andreas David Rosenberger (1857-1926)**, also from Kirchheim am Neckar. They had nine children, of which five did not survive infancy. There were seven girls and two boys, including a set of twins:

- Christiane Luise Rosenberger (1884-1884), aged about four months
- Christiane Katharine Rosenberger (1886-1953), aged almost 58 years
- Luise Maria Rosenberger (1887-1887), aged about four months
- Friederike Marie Rosenberger (1888-1932), aged 43 and a half years
- Female baby Rosenberger (1889-1889), died at birth
- David Gottlob Rosenberger (1891-1964), aged 73 years
- Marie Karoline Rosenberger (1892-1893) aged one year
- David Rosenberger (1895-1895), twin of Luise Marie, aged five months
- Luise Marie Rosenberger (1895-1980), twin of David, aged 85 years.

Their youngest child was **Luise Marie Rosenberger (1895-1980)**, who married Eugen Schmid and was the mother of **Käthe Schmid**. I met my third cousin, Käthe Greiner nee Schmid, in 2012 and am very grateful to her for sharing her memories, photographs, letters and stories with me. She is now in her mid-nineties (2024) and has two daughters and a number of grandchildren and great-grandchildren, who no longer live locally.

The American Connection

Three of Johann Jakob Trefz senior's children settled in Connecticut in the United States of America and another visited them a number of times before returning to Germany destitute and where he died penniless in 1924. **Georg Friedrich Trefz (1853-1919)** emigrated to America in 1880. **Rosina Katharina Trefz (1840-1910)** and her sister **Christine Sophia Trefz (1856-1906)** followed him less than a year later, sailing on the ship: 'Wieland' in 1881.

Georg Friedrich (Fritz) worked for at time for the royal household of the king of Württemberg. He started as a servant or labourer (*Hofknecht*) 2nd class in 1873 and moved on to 1st class in 1875 after a period of military service. He was sacked in 1880 for insubordination (*wegen Unbotmäßigkeit*). In June of the same year, he sailed for America. In America, Fritz worked at various jobs according to census and Connecticut city records, including as a collector of life insurance premiums, a cabinet maker, a crockery decorator, but for many years he was an employee of E Miller & Co, who manufactured brass fittings and fixtures for gas and electric lights. His sister, Rosina Katharina, looked after the house in which they both lived.

Christine Sophia married Wilhelm Immanuel Mayer (1862-1941) in Connecticut in 1883. She had arrived in the USA two years earlier with her sister, Katharina. Wilhelm Immanuel was born in Hochdorf, a small village not far from Hochberg, where Johann Jakob Trefz senior had moved to after being expelled from the Templers at the Kirschenhardthof. So it is possible that Christine and Wilhelm Immanuel knew each other in Germany or that there was at least some connection between the two families. Immanuel arrived in America in 1880 or 1881 and worked as a painter, joiner and cabinet maker. They could also have come to know each other in Connecticut as the men in the two families worked in similar industries and the German immigrant community would have known each other.

Christine and Immanuel had seven children:

- Emil Eugene Mayer (1883–1957), aged 74 years;
- **Emma Sophia Mayer (1885–1985),** aged 100 years;
- Friedrich (Fred) Gottlieb Mayer (1887–1979), aged 92 years;
- Elfrieda Louise Mayer (1889–1986), aged 97 years;
- Frank E Mayer (1890–1934), aged 44 years;
- Henry Ernst Mayer (1893–1968), aged 75 years;

- Lillian Wilhelmina Mayer (1895–1993), aged 98 years.

Although Christina died in 1906, she and Immanuel's children married and raised a tribe of children, grandchildren, and great grandchildren, with the exception of Frank Mayer, who was in the US military and seems to have died at the age of 44 after being hit by a train.

Christine and Wilhelm Immanuel's oldest daughter, **Emma Sophia Mayer (1885-1985)** lived to be 100 years old. She married twice but outlived both husbands, who died at an early age. She had only one child, a son, **William Parker Weaver (1911-1990)**.

After the Second World War, Emma had the Red Cross search for her German Trefz relatives, particularly those who had been in Palestine, i.e. those descended from my great grandfather, Johann Christoph Trefz (1849-1895). They eventually found my grandfather Fritz Trefz and my great uncle Wilhelm Trefz in an internment camp in Tatura, Australia. They continued to correspond for many years, until my grandfather passed away in 1954 when the contact between the families was lost for about 30 years. We still have copies of my grandfather's letters to Emma, thanks to her grandson, Bill **(William Frederick)** Weaver, but unfortunately, her letters to him have been lost.

Bill is a keen family historian and I am very grateful to him for helping me unlock the many mysteries of my Trefz family tree and sharing with me countless resources, stories and photographs for almost 15 years. Bill Weaver has two sisters and two children, and now several grandchildren. He has been researching his family history for over 40 years and even corresponded with my mother's first cousins in Australia: Annemarie (Amei) and Hartmann Trefz and my uncle Karl Georg Trefz (1918–2007) during the 1980s.

Johann Jakob Trefz junior (1845-1924), was the last surviving child from Johann Jakob senior's first marriage. He visited siblings in Connecticut a number of times and also worked there. According to Connecticut city records, he was in Meriden in 1883, and 1903 to 1908 and worked as a labourer or unskilled worker. He also had a valid German passport from 1887 to 1892, which is still in the hands of the American Trefz descendants. Johann Jakob junior returned to Germany some time before 1920, where he died penniless in 1924. In 1920, he wrote a letter to his nephew, Andreas David Rosenberger, about the Last Will and Testament of Fritz Trefz in America who had died the previous year. Jakob complained bitterly, saying that nothing at all should go to the *"Ostheimer Tante"* when he himself needed the money so much more than she did and that she was only related by marriage in any case.

An aunty from Ostheim *"die Ostheimer Tante"*

Johann Jakob Trefz senior's youngest child (from his second marriage), **Johann Christian Trefz (1857–1912)**, was born in 1857 and moved to Mannheim in Baden, where he worked as a metalworker/fitter and turner (*Schlosser*). How he came to move there is not known but perhaps he went there to do an apprenticeship under a master tradesman.

In Mannheim, in 1887, at the age of 30 years, he married Elisabetha Berg nee Baum (1854-1925), the widow of his former employer and *Sclossermeister*, Carl Ludwig Caspar Berg (1850-1882). Elisabetha was born in Essingen near Landau in Baden, the daughter of Johann Jakob Baum and Margaretha Walther. I'm told she spoke Swabian with a rather strange accent as she came from Baden[55]. She had had one child with her first

55 Personal communication Käthe Greiner per letter December 2014

husband, Carl Berg, but little Anna Berg only lived three and a half months. Carl Berg had six children with his first wife but only one of these, a son, survived more than a few years. So Elisabetha brought a stepson, Joseph Berg, into her marriage with Johann Christian Trefz.

Christian Trefz and Elisabetha had a son **Willi Oskar Trefz (1892-1917)** born on 3 August 1992. He was a soldier of the Kaiser (Wilhelm 2) in the Great War. At the age of 22, in June 1915, he was wounded at Bellwaarde-Ferme in Flanders, Belgium and later died of his wounds in 1917. Willi lies buried in a mass grave at Langemark, Flanders.

Johann Christian's family moved to Ostheim[56], a working class suburb of Stuttgart. Ostheim was established in the 1890s as a model workers community for labour needed for the nearby industrial factories. It is posible that Christian moved his family there in search of more stable work and / or a better situation for his family. It is likely that the housing there was newer and of better quality than what they had had in Mannheim. His wife, Elisabetha, was known in the family as 'die Ostheimer Tante' (the aunty from Ostheim)[57].

Willi Trefz around the beginning of WW1.

Johann Christian died in 1912 at the age of 55 years. Elisabetha died in 1925 at the age of 91 years and their only son, Willi, died in World War 1. With Willi's death, so ended another branch of the Trefz family.

56 Personal from communication Käthe Greiner, May 2012

57 ibid,

5. Johann Christoph goes to the Holy Land

While Johann Jakob Trefz senior never made it to the Holy Land, his son and my great-grandfather, **Johann Christoph (1849-1895)** did in 1869[58]. He was about 20 years old at the time. Little is known about exactly how and when Christoph got to Palestine. Most early Templers travelled to the Holy Land in groups of families and individuals in so-called *Wanderzüge*[59] (group migrations). These *Wanderzüge* left Germany several times a year in the early years of Templer settlement of the Holy Land. The members of each group were listed in "*Die Warte*". The "*Warte*" (the Sentinal), called variously *Süddeutsche Warte (until 1877)* and *Warte des Tempels*'. It was published by the Templers from 1845 and continues to the present day. In the 19th century, it contained religious and philosophical commentary as well as articles on the political situation in various parts of the world. As the *Süddeutsche Warte*, it was even subtitled: '*religöses u. politisches Wochenblatt*' (religious and political weekly paper). Community notices, such as births, deaths and marriages, played a lesser role in the very early *Warte*, although there are regular reports on migrations to Palestine and news from the colonies including the comings and goings of individual members.

The early Templers travelled overland and by boat or barge along the River Danube. Some crossed the sea from somewhere like Trieste to Alexandria in Egypt and onto Jaffa. Some also

58 See Johann Christoph's entry in Johann Jakob Trefz' parish register entry

59 Ibid. Personal communication from Peter Lange, Templer historian, 2012

travelled from Istanbul to Beirut in Lebanon (then a part of Syria) and onto Haifa or Jaffa before moving on to inland colonies, like Jerusalem. Most early Templers landed by ship in Haifa or Jaffa. As Jaffa had no deep-water port, passengers and cargo were offloaded onto small boats well into the 20th century when a deep water port was eventually built at Tel Aviv.

Although, there is no record of Christoph Trefz having been part of any Templer group migration[60], he may still have been part of one or he may have travelled alone. Johann Christoph's name does not appear in the 1869 "Warte" as part of an official Templer Wanderzug to the Holy Land[61]. While Christoph lived in Jerusalem until his death in 1895, there was no actual Templer colony there until 1873. He probably landed in Jaffa and may well have lived there for some time before the Jerusalem colony was built. On the other hand, just like individuals and Templer families lived in other towns and cities where there were no Templer settlements, Christoph may also have lived in the old city of Jerusalem before 1873. In any case, he moved to the Jerusalem German colony on the Rephaim plain outside the old city at some point. Here he had a house built and in 1881 married my great grandmother, Katharina Graf (1857-1916). I have not been able to find out exactly where this house was, but it must have been somewhere close to the Messerle family house in Beit Lehem Road in the German Colony, given the close relationship between the two families.

Stepsisters go to the Holy Land

In November 1873, **Katharina Graf (1857-1916)** and her stepsister Dorothea Adrion (1851-1891) travelled to Palestine with

60 Personal communication with Peter Lange 2012

61 Ibid. Personal communication from Peter Lange, Templer historian, 2012

a group of Templers as part of the fourth Templer Wanderzug[62]. Katharina was born in 1857 in Peterzell, a small rural village in the Black Forest, south of Stuttgart, as the 10th daughter of **Matthias Graf (1816-1865)** and his first wife, **Dorothea Seckinger (1817-1859)**. Dorothea died when Katharina was two years old as a result of complications with the birth of her 11th child, who also died.

In the same year, Katharina's father married again; a widow[63] named Dorothea Adrion née Wößner, who brought her eight year old daughter Dorothea Adrion into the marriage with her. The two stepsisters, Katharina Graf and Dorothea Adrion, grew up together and later travelled to the Holy Land together as young single women to make new lives there, initially landing in the Jaffa Templer colony[64] and later in living and marrying in Jerusalem.

Neuweiler, 10 gehen nach Jaffa, nemlich: Gustav Schiel mit Frau und Schwiegermutter und 2 Kindern von Kleingartach; die ledigen: Dorothea Adrian und Katharine Graf von Freudenstadt, Christine Rentschler aus Garrweiler, Christian Ha-

Even today, the Black Forest is made up of small rural communities. It is a thick, dark fir forest, which has a very claustrophobic feel about it. In the mid-19th century, these communities were even more remote and isolated than they are today. The people were mainly farmers and wood cutters and religion had a central place in their lives. Going to church, prayer and reading from the bible were fundamental

---

62 Personal communication from Peter Lange, Templer historian, 2013

63 A contemporaneous document indicates that Dorothea Adrion was illegitimate and therefore Dorothea Wößner and Jakob Adrion were not actually married.

64 Ibid. Personal communication from Peter Lange, Templer historian, 2013.

to their lives. In 2012, I spent a few days with relatives of my grandmother Aichele in Neuweiler, in the depths of the Black Forest, to find that prayer at mealtimes and reading from the Bible was still a thing in these parts.

In the 19th century, the Black Forest was also a hot-bed of religious rebellion and the centre of pietism. Templer thoughts and beliefs gained a strong foothold in these small rural communities with many families joining the German Temple (*Deutscher Tempel*) with numerous émigrés to Palestine coming from the countless small towns and villages in the Black Forest. So, it is no surprise that two young women found themselves called upon to help create God's kingdom on Earth in the Holy Land and went on a huge adventure to find husbands and make new lives in Jerusalem.

Dorothea Adrion married the shoemaker, Christian Messerle in Jerusalem in 1877. She bore him eight children before dying in 1891. He then married Pauline Buchhalter only to have 10 more children with her.

Dorothea Adrion and Christian Messerle

Christian Messerle built a house near the Templer precinct (*Saal* or community hall, secondary boys school and administrative headquarters) in the German colony in Jerusalem to house his growing family, partially with funds (4,000 Marks) inherited from his first wife Dorothea Adrion[65] upon her death.

65 Messerle inheritance documents from the German Consulate in Jerusalem now located in the Israeli National Archives in Jerusalem

This house is still standing today (2024) and is being run as a Bed and Breakfast guesthouse known as the Templer Inn. They have a wall of photographs showing the history of the Messerle family.

The Christian Messerle house in the German Colony of Jerusalem, now 'The Templer Inn'.

The Trefz and Messerle families have remained close down the generations; Katharine Trefz, was known in the Messerle family as 'Tante Trefz' (aunty Trefz) and she is pictured at a family wedding in 1906[66] (page 50). Dorothea's daughter Lina Messerle later became best friends with my grandmother, Anna Barbara Aichele.

This photo of 'Tante Trefz' (my great grandmother Katharina Trefz nee Graf) at the Fritz Buchalter/Maria Messerle wedding came from the daughter of Lina Messerle, Charlotte Weller Dravenieks nee Asenstorfer (1920-2014), who shared it with me, as well as many memories of her family and life in Jaffa in the 1920s and 1930s.

66 Tante Katharina Trefz at Buchhalter/Messerle wedding in 1906 in Jerusalem, scanned from the original owned by Charlotte Dravenieks née Messerle.

In 1881, Katharina Graf married **Johann Christoph TREFZ (1849-1895)** in Jerusalem and by 1899 she had given birth to five children, all boys:

- Jakob Matthias (1882-1904), aged 22.5 years;
- Christoph Gottlieb (1883-1966), aged almost 83 years;
- My grandfather, **Friedrich (Fritz) Christian TREFZ (1885-1954)**, aged almost 70 years;
- Carl August (1887-1959), aged 72 years; and
- Wilhelm Hermann (1889-1959), aged almost 70 years).

This is the only photograph[67] of my great grandfather, Johann Christoph Trefz that has survived. It is a studio portrait from about 1884 of Christoph (senior) and Katharina and their two eldest sons, Jakob Matthias and Christoph Gottlieb. There are no more photos until around 1910, when the boys are adults and Johann Christoph has long since died.

This may be because after my great grandfather's death in 1895, Katharina and her sons were too poor to spend money

67 Photo owned by Käthe Greiner, Kirchheim an Neckar, photographed by Anne Eckstein 2012

Johann Christoph Trefz, his wife and their two eldest sons: Gottlieb circa 1884.

on luxuries, such as studio portraits. Perhaps, there was also the shame that Christoph's suicide[68] had brought on the family.

Given the way that Katharina is holding the baby (Christoph Gottlieb), it is likely that she is pregnant with her third child, my grandfather *Fritz* (Friedrich Christian Trefz 1885–1954).

Debt and Suicide

Christoph Trefz (senior) was a businessman in Jerusalem; he was either a miller or a butcher, possibly both. In the family stories, he was a miller and owned a flour mill. Also, the church records from Kirchheim am Neckar, which have a

68 File of suicides from 1895-1901 now located in the Israeli National Archives in Jerusalem including the file on the 1893 lawsuit of Panisel versus Trefz from the German Consulate in Jerusalem.

later addition by his second son, Christoph Gottlieb, say his occupation was miller[69]. However, the mill in the Jerusalem colony in the late 19th century was owned by the Frank[70] family and a number of documents from the German Consulate in Jerusalem from 1892 to 1895 refer to his occupation as master butcher (*Metzgermeister*)[71]. In any case, he owned a business, or possibly two, as well as a house and seems to have been reasonably prosperous, at least for a time.

The story[72] about Christoph's suicide that has been handed down through the family is that while drunk in a tavern, Christoph signed away ownership of his flour mill to some Armenians. The Armenians challenged him to prove that he was not drunk by signing his name on a piece of paper. The paper was actually a deed of sale for the mill. When he turned up to the mill the next day, he was turned away by the 'new owners'. When he complained to the Turkish authorities, they refused to intervene because he confirmed that it was his signature on the document. In despair over what he had done, he committed suicide.

However, several documents dating from the 1890s, now housed in the Israeli National Archives, tell another story. All these documents say that Christoph was a master butcher; furthermore, the most significant document says that he had major debts; that he failed to pay what he owed and was subject to a lengthy lawsuit in 1893, involving both the German and Austro-Hungarian consulates in Jerusalem.

---

69 Ibid. Footnote 64

70 The miller, Matthaeus Frank (1846-1923) and his wife Gertrude built the first house in the colony in 1873. He also built the first steam-driven flour mill and ran a bakery in Emek Refa'im Street, opposite the site for the Templer community and administration centre. There were only windmills for grinding wheat before this.

71 Ibid. Footnote 67.

72 Personal communication per Hartmann Trefz, 2011

The Ottoman authorities generally didn't concern themselves with the civil and legal disputes of foreigners living in their empire and usually left such disputes to their consular officials to resolve.[73] I am now convinced that the story handed down within the family is a fiction, made up to lay blame somewhere else and that the real cause of his tragic death was despair over his debts and to escape his sizable financial problems.

An austro-hungarian citizen named Ascher Panisel, claimed a Christian (sic), (actually Christoph) Trefz owed him substantial monies for meat that had been ordered; a sum of 4804 ½ Piaster[74]. This would have been an enormous sum of money for the time. The German and Austro-Hungarian consular officials heard the case and determined Trefz was responsible for paying the debt. A repayment plan of monthly instalments of 811 ½ Piaster for the debt and the court costs was set up by the 'court' but Christoph never paid Panisel any money. He claimed the debt was actually incurred by a junior employee without authority and for which he personally was in no way responsible.

In her statement about her husband's suicide, his wife, Katharina, said[75] that in the weeks before his death, Christoph was becoming increasingly depressed (*von gedrückter Stimmung und Schwermuth*). He hardly spoke, rarely answered questions and spent his time doing bills and accounts. As he became increasingly aware of his unfortunate circumstances, Christoph became more and more withdrawn. He planned to return to Germany, possibly to borrow money. He had applied for a passport from the German Consulate on the day before his death, but his mood had lightened only a little.

---

73 Personal communication Charlotte Dravenieks, March 2012

74 Ibid. file on the 1893 lawsuit of Panisel versus Trefz

75 Ibid. file of suicides from 1895-1901 from the German Consulate in Jerusalem

Grave marker placed 2016.

On 21 April 1895 Johann Christoph Trefz committed suicide by hanging himself from an olive tree near the Templer colony in Jerusalem[76]. He lies buried in the Templer cemetery[77]. The grave is against the far right-hand wall on what would have been the extremities of the graveyard in 1895, surrounded by a low iron railing. There was not even a headstone. The location of the grave and the lack of a gravestone may have been because the cause of his death was suicide. In April 2016, after my second Templer trip to Israel, I was able to have a simple plaque placed on the grave on behalf of his descendants.

Life has to go on

After Johann Christoph's suicide, Katharina was left with five children aged between six and 13 years to raise and presumably also his debts to deal with. She had a small shop opposite the Templer school in Jerusalem, where she sold sweets, toys and knickknacks to the children of the colony. There

76 Ibid. file of suicides from 1895-1901 from the German Consulate in Jerusalem

77 Photograph of Johann Christoph Trefz' grave in the Templer Cemetry in Jerusalem by Anne Eckstein in May 2012

are no remaining pictures of Katharina or the boys as children, which is understandable given their reduced circumstances. Although by the time she made her last will and testament[78] in 1908, she had amassed some assets valued at 9800 Piaster, including a house in the Jerusalem Templer colony, a share in land in the Wilhelma colony and a shop as well as a relatively small debt of 3660 Piaster. This left net assets of 6140, a not inconsiderable achievement, given the situation she was left in just 13 years earlier.

In 1908, Katharina went into the *Diakonissen Hospital*[79] in Jerusalem to have an operation that she believed she would almost certainly not survive. The *Kaiserswerther Diakonissen* were protestant nuns, who had schools and hospitals in the Holy Land until World War 2. As my great grandmother was no longer physically able to attend the German Consulate in Jerusalem in person, Katharina Trefz nee Graf called consular officials to her bedside at the hospital to help her make her Last Will and Testament. (My own mother would later spend two years in her mid-teens "*in Stellung*" (somewhat similar to a work experience placement) working at this hospital, learning how to cook and clean.)

Katharina's will[80] provided for her estate to be divided among her four remaining sons. (Her oldest son, Jakob Matthias Trefz, had drowned after a stroke whilst in the German army on manoeuvres in Tauberscheckenbach, Germany on 18 September 1904.) She left her three sons: Christoph, a tailor in Frankfurt am Main; Fritz, a machine operator and fitter in

78 German Consulate in Jerusalem file of the Last Will and Testament of Katharina Trefz née Graf 1908-1916, now located in the Israeli National Archives in Jerusalem, transcribed by Anne Eckstein

79 Ibid Last Will and Testament of Katharina Trefz née Graf

80 Ibid Last Will and Testament of Katharina Trefz née Graf

Gaza; and Wilhelm, a salesman in Jerusalem, equal shares of 7/32nd parts of her estate. The remaining 11/32nd share, she left to her second youngest son, Karl, who was a blacksmith in Jerusalem at the time. (This is the same Karl Trefz who would eventually die penniless and destitute in Wildberg, Germany.) According to his mother's will, Karl was given a greater share because, because he was 'weaker and less capable of earning than his brothers'.

I suspect that this favouring of Karl over his brothers led to ongoing resentments by the others. Karl was hardly ever talked about by the Australian Trefz family, while Christoph was spoken about fondly and often, and letters were regularly exchanged, including with his widow, Mathilde, after his death.

Karl died in Germany in 1959 at the age of about 71 years. He was without means of support, living on the good will of the local community in an aged care home in Wildberg, near Calw in the Black Forest. With sizeable debts when he died, his brother Christoph disowned him and refused to take any responsibility for Karl's affairs for fear he would have to repay his debts as required under German law.

Katharina Trefz, nee Graf, died on the 1 January 1916, aged almost 59 years. It is not known whether she spent eight years in care, from 1908 to 1916, but I suspect she did. Her death notice in the '*Warte*' mentions a long and serious illness. In 1912, she was still in Jerusalem because her son Wilhelm sent a postcard from Jaffa to a cousin in Germany where he said that he had visited his mother in Jerusalem after returning to Palestine from Germany.

Mind you, by the time of her death, Wilhelm was living in Jaffa, as the death notice shows. If she was well enough to leave hospital, she may have lived with him in Jaffa. Wilhelm's son Hartmann Trefz told me that he believed she live with

Verwandten und Bekannten machen wir hiermit die schmerzliche Mitteilung, daß unsere innigstgeliebte, unvergeßliche Mutter, Schwiegermutter und Tante

Katharina Trefz

geb. Graf

nach langer, schwerer Krankheit im Alter von $58^{3}/_{4}$ Jahren am 1. Januar 1916 sanft entschlafen ist.

Im Namen der trauernden Hinterbliebenen

Wilhelm Trefz.

Jaffa, 1. Januar 1916.

Katharina Graf death notice from 'die Warte'

his parents in Jaffa. However, she still had the family house in Jerusalem when she died. Her sons, Fritz and Karl were working in Gaza, and Christoph Gottlieb was already living in Germany. She was probably not living in her house in Jerusalem by herself.

The four Trefz brothers (L to R): my great uncles Wilhelm, Karl, Christoph and my grandfather, Fritz Trefz.

6. The Trefz brothers

This is the first photograph of the remaining four Trefz' brothers as adults and dates from around 1907 or perhaps a little later. From left are Wilhelm Hermann (the youngest), Karl August, Christoph Gottlieb (the oldest) and Friedrich (Fritz) Christian, my grandfather.

Familiennachrichten.

Todes-Anzeige.

Verwandten und Bekannten gebe ich die schmerzliche Nachricht, daß mein geliebter Bruder

Jakob

am 13. September beim Baden, infolge Schlaganfalls, in Tauberscheckenbach ertrunken ist.

In tiefer Trauer:

Christoph Trefz.

Jakob Matthias (1882-1904), died aged 22 and a half years, when he had a stroke and drowned, while he was swimming in the Tauber-schenkenbach, where he was on manoeuvres doing military service.

Great uncle **Karl August Trefz (1887-1959)** died in Wildbad in the Black Forest, single and heavily indebted. In 1908, he was still in Jerusalem, working as a blacksmith. Exactly when and why he relocated to Germany is not known; it was probably just before or during the Great War. He had a document from the German Consulate approving his stay in Palestine for 1914. He doesn't seem to have been there during the 1920s and 1930s and doesn't appear in any later family pictures. Nothing much is known about his life, except that he was penniless and dependant on the charity of the local municipality of Wildberg when he died.

Christoph Gottlieb Trefz (1883-1966), my great uncle, returned to Germany and was living in Frankfurt am Main by 1908[81]. He was a tailor and had his own shop. He married Matthilde Sybilla Blatt and lived with her in Frankfurt until he died in 1966, aged 83 years. Matthilde died in an aged care home about 8 years later in 1974. They had no children.

As the oldest surviving son. Christoph Gottlieb, became head of the family. He made some additions and updates to the family entry in the church records in Kirchheim am Neckar. He seems to have kept an eye on his brother Karl, who became destitute in old age but disowned him, so that he wouldn't have to pay for Karl's debts.

Great uncle Wilhelm

Familiennachrichten
Anna Surber
Wilhelm Trefz
Verlobte.
Dielsdorf (Zürich) Jaffa Mai 1914. Jerusalem

My great uncle, Wilhelm Hermann Trefz (1889-1959) was a clerk and a salesman. He became a successful businessman in Jaffa, firstly working for Paul Aberle and later managing the Jaffa business once Aberle relocated to Jerusalem[82]. He also bought the Aberle house in Jaffa and was the only one of the four Trefz brothers to own their own home in Palestine.

At the age of 26, Wilhelm married Anna Surber (1887-1971) on 19 June 1915 in Jaffa, Palestine. Anna was a Swiss girl who had gone to Palestine with a girlfriend, who was to be

81 Ibid File of the Last Will and Testament of Katharina Trefz née Graf

82 Personal communication Hartmann Trefz, 2012

married to an Abyssinian prince[83]. The engagement fell through and the other girl returned home to Switzerland with Anna giving her the money for the fare. Anna remained in Palestine, where she worked at the Hotel Jerusalem in Jaffa to repay the money she had borrowed for her girlfriend's fare.

Once the British ousted the Turks from Palestine at the end of WW1, German nationals there were interned and transported to Egypt. In Egypt, the Templer women and later some of the men were interned at the Al Hayat Hotel (a converted sanatorium) in Heluan.

As a Swiss citizen, Anna was considered neutral and could have remained free. Nevertheless, she chose to follow the German women and children into internment in Heluan, where they were detained from July 1918 to December 1919. "*The men were at first interned elsewhere (in Cairo) and then some of the older men were released to join their families at the Al Hayat Hotel in Helouan.* [84]"

In December 1919, some people were repatriated to Germany and some were later released to return to their settlements in Palestine in September 1920.

Wilhelm and Anna Trefz were repatriated to Germany, where they lived in Hamburg for a time before returning to British Mandate Palestine around 1920. In 1924, William and Anna had a daughter, Anne Marie, known as 'Amei'. Five years later, in 1929, their son Hartmann was born.

---

83 Abyssinia is present-day Ethiopia. Hartmann Trefz, Wilhelm and Anna's son, told me this story.

84 Doris Frank, Christian Messerle Family, version 4, September 2017

Hartmann, Wilhelm, Amei and Anna Trefz in the early 1930s.

Although a time of unrest and despite curfews, Amei and Hartmann as well other Templers, spoke fondly of their youth in 1930s Palestine. There was much unrest between Arabs and Jews, especially as newly immigrated Jews created pressure for limited housing and jobs. Some Templer families moved to former German colonies in Africa at this time, such as in Tanganyika and started again. Those with either agricultural or town properties in Palestine, including Wilhelm Hermann Trefz and their families lived a relatively comfortable life for the times.

Anna and Hartmann Trefz with Swiss Consul in Jaffa, Carl Robert Lutz (1895-1975) and his wife Gertrud in front of Wilhelm Trefz' house in the Jaffa.

Wilhelm owned a house in Jaffa, as well held investments with the Templer Bank and a share in property in Sarona.

At the outbreak of WW2, on the same day (almost within the hour) that war was declared on 3rd Sept 1939, Wilhelm was taken into custody along with the other abled bodied adult German males in Jaffa. They were held overnight at a jailhouse in Jaffa, where wives could visit their imprisoned husbands. The next day, they were all taken to prison at *Akko* (Acre).

My great uncle Wilhelm is carrying a small suitcase in the picture below, taken when the British Palestinian police detained him. This little suitcase survived imprisonment in Akko, transportation on the Queen Elisabeth to Australia, internment at Tatura in country Victoria and the over 80 years since.

Wilhem Trefz taken into custody at the beginning of WW2 in Jaffa.

Templers living in the metropolitan settlements such as Jaffa and Walhalla were relocated and boarded with their families or friends in the rural colonies such as Sarona and Wilhelma. There the German internees could be more easily controlled and supervised by the British.

These agricultural colonies were simply surrounded by

barbed wire with the exits controlled by guards and just turned into large internment camps. While the many internees could live in their own homes, they had to take in displaced family and friends from the city. They were not allowed leave the 'camp' to tend their crops and animals and so had to pay Arab labourers to keep their farms going.

By World War 2, Anna Trefz nee Surber had relinquished her Swiss citizenship and was interned along with the rest of her family. In 1941, Amei and Hartmann, their parents Wilhelm and Anna, along with my grandfather Fritz were transported to Australia on the "Queen Elizabeth", which had been converted into a troop ship. They were finally interned at Tatura in country Victoria for the rest of the war and beyond.

Life after the internment camp was hard in a strange new land, especially for Wilhelm who had been a well to do businessman in Palestine. He had to take manual farm and factory work in Australia. The whole family took whatever work they could get; Anna and Amei did house-keeping and cleaning, and Hartmann did farm work before later going to the University in Melbourne to study Commerce.

Wilhelm Trefz and his family in the late 1950s

However hard things were in Australia, it was nowhere near as bad as it was in Germany after the war. There, people really had nothing. Some of the Templers interned at Tatura had elected to be repatriated to Germany after their release from internment. Among them was Wilhelm Messerle and his

Wilhelm Trefz Family home

family, a step cousin of Willhelm Trefz through his mother. Even though they had very little, Wilhelm and Anna Trefz still managed to send care packages of food, tea and coffee to Wilhelm Messerle's family in Germany in those early years after the war.

Wilhelm Trefz and his family moved to Victoria in the late 1940s where many other Templers were also settling. They made their home in McKinnon, quite close to where the Bentliegh-Moorabbin Templer community centre was later built. The family home at 39 Lees Street was a modest 1930s bungalow and was bought in September 1951 at a cost of 3100 Pounds. After a deposit of 800 Pounds, Hartmann and Amei took out the bank loan for 2300 Pounds because she had a clerical job and he worked at the bank. Wilhelm and Anna Trefz lived the rest of their lives in this house, as did Hartmann, until he moved into aged care in 2013, less than a year before he died at 84 years.

Amei and Ignaz marry at the Registry Office in 1972.

In 1972, at the age of 48, **Annemarie (Amei) Trefz (1924-1987)** married Ignaz Jakob Rügg (1914–2005), a Swiss national who had walked overland to Australia for the 1956 Melbourne Olympic Games to support the Swiss walking team. He stayed on, and a respectful year after her mother's death, Amei and Ignaz were married. Amei and Ignaz had been together for many years but her mother did not approve of her daughter marrying. She believed that it was Amei's duty to look after her mother until she died. Amei was a dutiful daughter and respected her mother's wishes. By the time Amei and Ignaz married, she was too old to have children. Amei was a gentle soul, who was always caring and compassionate to those around her. She would cook for Hartmann and clean the Lee Street house until a few weeks before her death from cancer.

Amei first worked as a housekeeper and cleaner in South Australia to help the family make ends meet after their release from internment. She later attended secretarial college and worked for many years as a secretary for the Temple Society of Australia in the Head Office in Bentleigh. Amei died of breast and liver cancer in 1987 at the age of 63 years. Ignaz survived her by another 18 years.

Hartmann as an adult

Hartmann Trefz (1929–2014) went to university and graduated with a Bachelor's Degree in Commerce from the University of Melbourne. He then became a bank officer and worked at the ANZ Bank until he retired. He was a shy man and lived a quiet life, living in the family home for over 63 years, until old age and frailty forced him to move into the TTHA (Templer and Tabulam Home for the Aged) late in 2013.

Hartmann in Arab costume.

Hartmann cared for family and community. He enjoyed playing tennis and fossicking for gold with a metal detector. He volunteered for the Temple Society and served on the TTHA Board. Although he had several romances during his lifetime, he never married and had no children. He suffered a massive stroke in 2014, passing away a few days later.

Hartmann Trefz at the TTHA in 2014

In his Will, Hartmann asked that his ashes be cast into the ocean. This proved to be more than a little challenging for my cousin Sigi Messner, who as executor of the estate, was charged with carrying out this important responsibility.

Sigi had planned to throw the ashes into the Mediterranean Sea whilst on a cruise, but that is a sea, not an ocean. Also, special permission would be needed to take the canister of ashes onto every plane and transport it through every country on its way to its final resting place. The solicitor did not approve!

Similarly, Port Phillip Bay (a bay, not an ocean), Bass Strait (a strait), and the Tasman Sea were also ruled out. Another complication was that it is against the law of the sea to throw ashes from a ship and most captains of larger ships and cruise liners won't allow it.

Finally, a plan was hatched to charter a fishing boat, sail off the coast of northern New South Wales to where the Pacific Ocean begins, and dispose of the ashes there. The solicitor finally approved and the GPS location of the exact spot was duly sent to him as verification.

Opa Fritz

My grandfather, **Friedrich (Fritz) Christian Trefz (1885-1954)**, married **Anna Barbara Aichele (1889-1930)** in Jerusalem in 1910. Fritz was a tradesman, a metalworker. He worked in various places around Palestine and the Lebanon, then a part of Syria. In Beirut, he met his future wife, Anna Barbara Aichele, who was working at the Hotel Gassmann, one of the finest German hotels in the orient at the time. Their children were born in Gaza, Jerusalem and Jaffa, except for Karl who was born in Neuweiler, Germany during WW1.

Anna Barbara Aichele married Fritz Trefz in 1910.

The Hotel Gassmann in Beirut

From Neuweiler in the Black Forest, Anna Barbara was born the eldest but illegitimate child of Catharina Aichele. At the age of 15 years, she left home and family to travel alone to the Middle East to work in the kitchens of the Proβ (Pross) Guesthouse which later became the prestigious Hotel Gassmann in Beirut.

The position was most likely arranged for her through the Proβ family in Neuweiler who are distantly related to the Aichele's, and whose descendants Friedrich and Johannes Proβ, owned a guesthouse, which later became the Hotel Gassmann.

Anna Barbara Trefz in 1910

Ernst August Gassmann (1866-1921), rebuilt and expanded the guesthouse in 1907. It had a reputation for being one of the best hotels in the region well into the mid 1920s. The Gassmann family is also connected to the Prosses of Neuweiler through the wife of one of Ernst August Gassmann's sons. This may explain why Anna Barbara was allowed to travel so far away at such a young age. Mind you, a 15-year old at that time would have already been in the workforce.

By all accounts, Anna Barbara was a strong woman. She grew up in the shadow of her mother's scandalous behaviour as an unwed mother in a small village in the Black Forest where everyone knew everyone else. After Anna Barbara married Fritz Trefz, they lived in Gaza for a time, where Willy (Wilhelm) Friedrich, (1911-1919) was born. She had four more children, three in Palestine and one in Neuweiler in Germany.

Anna Barbara and Fritz had five children:

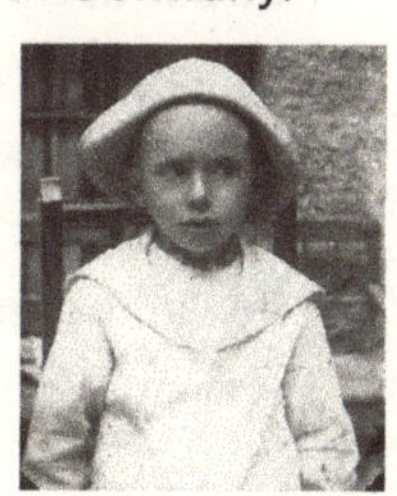

Willy Trefz in Neuweiler where he died.

- **Wilhelm (Willy) Friedrich, (1911-1919)** was born in Gaza and died at the age of 8 years in 1919 in Calw, Germany
- **Otto Christoph (1912-1987)** was born in Jerusalem, perhaps in the family home owned by Fritz and Katharina Trefz nee Graf

- Ida Katharina **(1914-2004)** was also born in Jerusalem
- My mother, **Elisabeth (Elli) Gertrud (1916-1988)** was born in Jaffa, where the midwife lived
- **Karl Georg (1918-2007)**, the youngest, was born in Neuweiler after an epic overland journey back to Germany in the middle of the Great War.

Ida Trefz, aged about 2 years

Back to the Black Forest

In late 1916, in the midst of the First World War, the Trefz family returned to Germany. With all the things they could put in a small cart *(Leiterwagen)* and with four young children in tow. My mother was the youngest, having been born in February 1916. The family travelled overland by various means to Damascus, then to Istanbul and on into Europe. From Romania they caught the train back to Germany to live with Anna Barbara's family in the large family farmhouse in Neuweiler in the Black Forest.

The story I remember from my mother was that my grandmother, Anna Barbara, made this journey alone with the children, who ranged in ages from less than one year to about five years old. Fritz may have been there as well and by 1917 he was working at *Daimler Motoren Gesellschaft* in Germany. Later the family moved to the nearby city of Calw, where they lived until returning to Palestine in about 1920 to live in rented premises next to several other Templer families just outside to old city of Jaffa.

Anna Barbara Trefz, nee Aichele (1880-1930) died of cancer in 1930 at the age of only 51 years.

She was seen by the German doctors at the *Diakonissen Hospital* in Jerusalem, who couldn't treat her and sent her to a clinic in Tübingen in Germany.

She returned to Germany without her family and without the younger children really understanding the seriousness of her illness. In Tübingen, the doctors said that the cancer was already too far advanced, so she went to live with her uncle Georg Sebastian Aichele and his family in Pfullingen, where she died six weeks later.

The Trefz children never saw their mother again after she didn't return from cancer treatment in Germany. My mother, **Elisabeth (Elli) Gertrud Trefz (1916-1988)**, was only 14 at the time and it greatly affected her for the rest of her life. She never really dealt with it.

Anna Barbara Trefz, already very ill, just before returning to Germany for treatment.

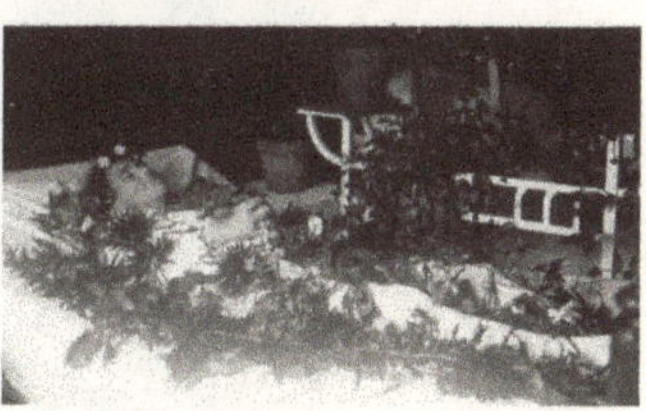

My grandmother, Anna Barbara Trefz on her deathbed.

The Trefz children after learning of the death of their mother.

L-R: Anna Barbara Aichele nee Klink, Anna Barbara Trefz nee Aichele as a child and Catharina Aichele about 1885

7. The Aichele's from the Black Forest

A Long Line of Stonemasons

The Aichele family have lived in Neuweiler in the Black Forest for many generations. **Christoph Wilhelm Aichele (abt 1730–1798)** was born in Neuweiler but the family may have come from Deckenpfonn before that. I have not been able to find any ancestors there as yet though. Another task I shall leave to another generation.

He was a stone mason *(Maurer)* and my 5th great grandfather on my mother's side. He married **Magdalenna Schwämml or Schwemml (Abt 1736-unknown)** and they had at least six children together, but not all of them survived to adulthood:

- Magdalena (1769-unknown);
- **Sebastian (1771-1808)** aged 37 years and my 4th great grandfather;
- Anna Catharina (1773-1837);
- Male (1775-1775) aged only one day old;
- Female (1777-1777) aged only one day old; and
- Male (1779-1779) aged only one day old.

Sebastian Aichele, my 4th great grandfather, was a master stone mason (*Maurermeister*) in Neuweiler. He married **Catharina Proß (1879–1848)** and they had seven children:

- Sebastian junior (1794-sometime before 1802), aged no more than eight years;
- Maria Magdalena (1797-unknown);
- **Johann Martin (1798-1867)**, aged 69 years and my 3rd great grandfather;
- Anna Maria (1800-1864), aged 64 years;

- Sebastian junior (1802-unknown);
- Christina Catharina (1804-unknown); and
- Jakob (1805-1810), aged five years.

Johann Martin was my 3rd great grandfather and also a master stone mason like his father and grandfather before him. He married **Magdalena Roller (1797–1864)** in 1823 and they had five children that we know of:

- Anna Maria (1824-1913), aged nine years;
- Sebastian (1825-1825), about three months;
- Elisabeta (1828-1828), about five months;
- Elisabetha (1829-1894), aged 65 years;
- **Georg Friedrich (1838-1887)**, aged 49 years, my 2nd great grandfather.

Georg Friedrich married **Anna Barbara Klink (1840–1922)** and they had 11 children, three of whom died in infancy and another two never married:

- Johann Michael Aichele (1864-1864), died at about one week;
- Elisabetha Aichele (1865-1920); married with five children and died aged 55 years;
- Johann Georg Aichele (1867-1895), remained single and continued to live in the family home in Neuweiler until he died aged 28 years;
- My great-grandmother, **Catharina Aichele (1868-1943)**, had three illegitimate children and lived at home until she died aged 75 years;
- Magdalena 'Madele' Aichele (1870-1907), married with five children and died aged 37 years[85];
- Friedrich Aichele (1872-1921) married in the United States of America, had six children and died there aged 49 years;
- Georg Sebastion Aichele (1873-unknown) married and moved to his wife's home town of Pfullingen, where they

85 Her husband, Samuel Mast, remarried two more times after Magdalena's death and had another child with each of these wives

had three children, although I only remember two of them being talked about in the family;

- Martin Aichele, (1876-1955) travelled the world working in high end hotels and late married and lived in Berlin, where he died aged 79 years;
- Anna Maria (1877-1878), died at just over 12 months;
- Samuel Aichele (1880-1908), remained single, living at home until he died at 28; and
- Georg Adam Aichele (1882-1886) died aged 4 years.

Despite their large family, Catharina's parents were considered reasonably prosperous. They owned a substantial farmhouse, which is now (2012) divided into a number of apartments. They also owned farmland, pastures, a section of forest, and above all horses, which was a sign of wealth[86].

Scandal in the family

My great grandmother, **Catharina Aichele (1868-1943)** grew up in a family of 11 children in the small village of Neuweiler in the Black Forest. She never married but had three children by at least two different men, who both promised to marry her.

Great grandmother Catharina Aichele about 1918

My grandmother, **Anna Barbara Aichele (1889–1930)** was her first child. She had two more children; firstly, Friedrich (1897-1897), who died as a baby, and then Georg Samuel Aichele (1900-1965) who married and raised his family in Neuweiler.

86 Personal communication, Margarete Nestel nee Hummel, 2011

Catharina was as tough as old nails. She withstood the scandal of living as an unmarried mother in her small community of perhaps 400-500 people at the end of the 19th century. Her family stood by her and she was able to raise her children in the family home at Hofstetter Straβe 8 in Neuweiler.

Catharine Aichele with niece Katharina Kübler nee Mast and baby, and granddaughter Maria Aichele

Catharina worked as a leading hand, managing a team of woodcutters / farm workers in the forest. She continued to live in the family home with her brothers Johann Georg, Martin and Samuel, and later with her sister Magdalena's family until her death in 1943 at the age of 75 years. The original door to the house, now leads to the cellar. The house was built in 1850, as inscribed on the beam above the door,

Great grandmother, Catharina Aichele (marked with an 'X') in the Black Forest making hay.

In 1897, Catharina Aichele had a second child, Friedrich Aichele, with a different father, but he only lived about three months.

Great grandmother, Catharina Aichelel, with son Georg Samuel and family.

A few years later, she had another child, Georg Samuel Aichele (1900-1965), presumably with the second father. Samuel grew up in Neuweiler, where he married Anna Barbara Heselschwerdt (1903-1995). They had two daughters: **Frieda (born 1925)** and **Maria (1928-2012)**. Maria married a local man, Erwin Schöttle whose family still operate a transport/trucking business in Neuweiler. Frieda married Kurt Kühnle and they had one daughter, **Karin**, who now lives in Kornwestheim with her aging mother.

Elisabetha Aichele (1865-1920) married Konrad Keinath and they had five children, **Friedrich, Rosel (Rösle), Friedrich Wilhelm, Gustav Adolf** and **Konrad**. They lived in Onsmettingen, Stuttgart. My mother continued to write to her 'Tante Rösle' (actually her first cousin once removed) for many years from Australia.

Magadalena (Madele) Aichele (1870-1907) married Samuel Mast (1870-1924) but she died quite young at the age of 37. They had five children:

- Barbara (died at one week);
- Johann (Hans) Georg (1898-unknown);
- Friedrich (died at two weeks);
- Rosina (1900-1956); and
- Katharina (1902-1956).

After Madele's death, Samuel Mast remarried two more times and had another child with each of these women. He had Samuel Mast Jun. with his second wife, Christiane Adam, who died in childbirth. Samuel soon married again and had Philipp Mast with his third wife, Katharina Lörcher (1873–1961). Katharina was instrumental in raising the children from all three marriages, even though her own son, Philipp Mast, died aged two years.

Samuel's eldest daughter, **Katharina Mast (1902-1956)**, married Johann Michael Kübler. Katharina was one of my mother Elli Trefz' godparents, when my grandmother had the remaining children[87] baptised as a 'job lot' at the protestant church in Neuweiler after the youngest Karl was born in 1918. Katharina had four children: **Karl, Katharina, Georg** and **Wilhelm**. Her son Georg Kübler and his wife Hilde (who died 2016) have lived in an apartment in the Aichele family farmhouse in Neuweiler for many years. They have no children. I stayed with them for a few days in 2012 and they generously shared many family stories, pictures and memories with me.

Katharine's older sister, **Rosine Mast (1900-1956)** married Gottlieb Kling. They had a daughter Erika, who married and had five children. I have no information about **Johann (Hans) Georg Mast (1898-unknown)**, Katharina's older brother.

The Aichele family farmhouse was still standing at Hofstetterstrasse 8 in Neuweiler when I visited in 2012 and Georg Kübler, pictured on facing page, was still living there:

A Brawler flees the country

Catharina's younger brother **Friedrich Aichele (1871-1920)** escaped to America in 1895. The family story is that he was involved in a pub brawl where a man was stabbed to death.

87 Willy and Otto were not baptised as they had been 'presented' in the Templer 'Saal" in Palestine.

Friedrich was accused of the crime but before he could be arrested and carted off to jail, he fled the country to the United States of America. He settled in Hudson County, New York State, where he married Christina Hettesheimer and they had six children. Some of those children visited their German family in the Black Forest in the late 1920s and 1930s. However, Friedrich himself never returned to his German homeland for fear of arrest. He was ultimately proven innocent when the real killer confessed to the crime on his death bed.

Georg Sebastion Aichele (1873–1951) married Maria Regine Groller and moved to Pfullingen, near Reutlingen. They had three children: **Richard, Berta and Johanna**, although I don't recall mention of Richard in the familiy. Richard married Katharine Frey and they had two children: **Richard Ernst** and

Rosemarie. Berta married Gerhard Keinath and had a son **Gustav**. Johanna married Walter Georg Hummel and had two daughters, **Margarete and Irmgard**. I spoke with Margarete shortly before her death in 2011 from cancer. She gave me a lot of information and told me the stories that I have retold here about her family.

Martin Aichele (1876-1955) worked for a large high-end international hotel chain. He worked in both London and New York and perhaps elsewhere.

Quite late in life, in 1918, he married Hedwig Wilhelmine Adolphine Harras from Weissensee in Berlin. They lived in Berlin for the rest of their lives, where he owned a house, but they had no children.

The house was in the Soviet sector after the war and was compulsorily acquired by the East German state after they died. After the fall of the Berlin Wall in 1989 lawyers contacted the descendants of the family in the West to attempt to reclaim the property. My brother Walter and I did not take part in these efforts.

Martin Aichele

Hedwig and Martin Aichele

8. Palestine between the Wars

Life in the Orient

My overwhelming memories about what I heard from parents, family and other Templers about Palestine in the 1920s and 1930s are that life was good. It wasn't always perfect; people had to rebuild their homes and businesses which had been looted and damaged through years of neglect during and after WW1. There was also unrest between Arabs and Jews from time to time, which had its dangers for other inhabitants. The British imposed a night-time curfew and blew up large areas of Jaffa where Arab insurgents were supposedly hiding. A large area in the middle of the old city of Jaffa is now parkland for this very reason. The economic situation was progressively deteriorating. This prompted some Templers to relocate to Tanganyika in Africa. British rule could be bureaucratic, but people mostly talked very fondly of those times. What follows are my impressions and recollections as shared by family, friends and other Templers who experienced it first hand:

Trefz family domestic help who almost became part of the family: Arive and her husband Arafat on the terrace of the Trefz home,

While life in Palestine was simple by today's standards, it was starting to change. Electricity was available to light homes and public buildings. A postal service to the Templer

The Trefz children in front of the Gemeindehaus in Jaffa in the early 1920s.

colonies was in place. Later on, some wealthier Templers could afford cars, while trucks and vans eventually replaced horses and carts. Even average families could afford Arab domestic servants to help with cooking, washing and cleaning, although cooking was still on a wood-burning or primus stove. Water was boiled in a wood-fired copper for washing clothes and for bathing. Templers also hired Arabs as agricultural workers on their farms and to help with the harvest. They were also employed as labourers in various businesses in the Templer colonies in towns and cities.

The Templers lived in a German language and cultural bubble in their colonies in the Holy Land, much as migrant communities do anywhere they go in the world, but perhaps with more rigour and enthusiasm than most. Religion, work and community life were fundamental. They had a community house or hall (*Gemeindehaus*) in each of their colonies for services (*Saal*), meetings and various social gatherings.

Templer Gemeindehaus in Jaffa in 2106

Protestant Immanuel Church in Jaffa

In Jaffa, there was also a German protestant church (now called the Immanuel church) as there were also numbers of non-Templer Germans in the community. My grandmother, Anna Barbara Trefz née Aichele, remained a protestant and both her daughters, Ida and Elli, were confirmed in the protestant church in Jaffa in 1930 just before she returned to Germany for cancer treatment. Older brother, Otto was also confirmed as a Templer.

Marriage was generally within the Templer community, or at least with other ethnic Germans or Austrians; more rarely with other Europeans. A cousin of Hartmann Trefz fell in love with and married a British policeman stationed in Palestine. She had come from Switzerland in the mid-1930s to help look after Hartmann because he was running a bit wild. She returned to England with her husband. Such relationships were relatively rare.

Confirmation of Ida and Elli Trefz in 1930

There were various leisure opportunities among Templer communities, including cafes and restaurants, dances and sports. At the Café Lorenz in Walhalla, there were dances and regular screenings of films. There was also the Arabic cinema, the Allhambra, in Jaffa. There were Templer sporting clubs in the German colonies, as well as sporting groups from other communities. Also, there were football (soccer) matches played against one another.

Swimming was very popular, given the climate and nearby beaches. The "*Südstrand*" in Jaffa was very popular and the "Villa *Südstrand*", an old mansion on the beach used as a sporting club, was a popular hangout for Templer young people. My father too, became a member there.

Andromeda rocks and *Adamsfelzen* at the *Südstrand* 2016

Swimming out to the Andromeda rocks, the reef around Jaffa, and to the "*Adamsfelsen*", the largest of the rocks, was a popular challenge of sporting ability. My aunt Ida Trefz was a strong swimmer and often talked about her swims to the rock and back.

Adamsfelzen – painted in 1938

The Templers took to the local food like a duck to water. Hummus, baba ganoush and flat bread '*Fladen*' were popular, cheap and readily available. Some even mastered the tricky skill of making baklava. Even today, many families still incorporate dishes inspired by Arab or Turkish traditions. I remember seeing this cabbage dish that my mother used to cook regularly when I was a child, and I still cook occasionally, on Rick Stein's 'Venice to Istanbul' television cooking program[88]. I had always thought it was from Germany. Now I know that it is actually a Turkish dish called *Kapuska*![89]

---

88 Rick Stein's 'Venice to Istanbul' program and cookbook, P.146

89 Mind you, there are probably some Balkan, Russian and Black Sea coast influences as well

On a Templer trip to Israel in 2016, there was an intense discussion on the best recipe for making *Maqlouba*, which literally means upside down, and is a one-pot dish made with rice, chicken and vegetables. (I don't think there was ever any agreement on the best method!) Tomato salad is commonly made with lemon juice (rather than vinegar), tahini, parsley and mint, much to the disapproval of my Aunt Lotte Trefz, who came from Thuringia and didn't care much for Templer oriental cuisine. "*Traubenwürstle*", unlike Greek *dolmades* are made with fresh vine leaves, not preserved ones, and lots of lemon juice.

Many Arabic words and phrases have also found their way into 'Templer German' and even into 'Templer English'. As a child, I always believed: *mishmish* actually "*mushamash*" (apricots), *bandora* actually "*bandura*" (tomatoes), *badiech* actually "*albatikh*" (watermelon), *gusa* actually "*kusa*" (zucchini) were German words. *Jala* (hurry up) is also a common term still used by some Templers, even those who have never been to Palestine. It is also not uncommon for the occasional Arabic swear word and curse to have survived.

In Jaffa, the Templers had a small hospital and a German doctor in the colony to take care of basic health needs. My great uncle, Wilhelm Trefz' house in Jaffa was next door to the hospital. In the Sarona colony, there was a pharmacy run by a German speaking Jew, Isidor Mamlok[90] For more serious health needs, Jerusalem had more facilities, including the German Kaisserwerther Diakonissen Hospital, which had firstly operated out of the Old City and by the late 1920s had moved to larger facilities in the *Prophetenstrasse*, (the street of the prophets) outside the walls of old Jerusalem.

---

90 *From Desert Sands to Golden Oranges: The History of the German Templer Settlement of Sarona in Palestine from 1871 to 1947*, by Helmut Glenk, in conjunction with Horst Blaich and Manfred Häring, 2005, Page 176

While the Templers initially established agricultural communities, they soon evolved into a complex economy. Farming (vegetables, grain, dairy, orchards) were important for food production and later for export or for sale to community members living in the towns and cities. Mills to grind flour, bakeries, and butcher shops soon followed. There were also builders, blacksmiths, engineering works, tile makers and mechanical workshops. Templers ran hotels, restaurants and cafes, transport and haulage businesses as well as retail shops and import-export businesses. Jaffa oranges were exported from Sarona back to Germany, while household goods, farming machinery and clothing were imported for the use of the colonists. There was even the Templer Bank to deal with savings, investments, insurance and other financial transactions for the colonies.

The Templers in Palestine ran their own schools according to the German curriculum; kindergarten, primary, and secondary schools. Kindergarten and primary school were offered in Jaffa. A secondary school was available in Sarona, three kilometres away, although later they were merged into a new school in Sarona. Girls generally completed primary school in the 1920s and 1930s. A Templer senior secondary school for boys was offered in Jerusalem.

Kinderschule Jaffa circa 1922: Elli and Karl Trefz marked with an 'X'.

At about 14, girls and boys were confirmed and had religious lessons. Girls then spent about two years *'in Stellung'* where they worked for a family or an employer, learning to cook, clean, look after children and keep house in preparation for marriage.

Boys completed primary school and some years of secondary school until learning a trade by completing an apprenticeship with a master tradesman or working on the family farm. For academically gifted students (i.e. boys), a final two years was offered at the lyceum in Jerusalem, which could lead on to university studies in Germany.

Strikes, riots, and curfews

In the mid-1930s, there was escalating unrest between Arabs and Jews in Palestine. There were strikes, protests and riots which unsettled the otherwise peaceful life of the Templers.

Ida and Elli sitting on the rubble in Jaffa in 1936.

The British were hard pressed to control the situation and introduced a curfew. A pass was needed to be out after dark. The Templers had little choice but to learn to live with it. My mother put together a whole photograph album of blown up buildings and streets in Jaffa from the unrest in 1936.

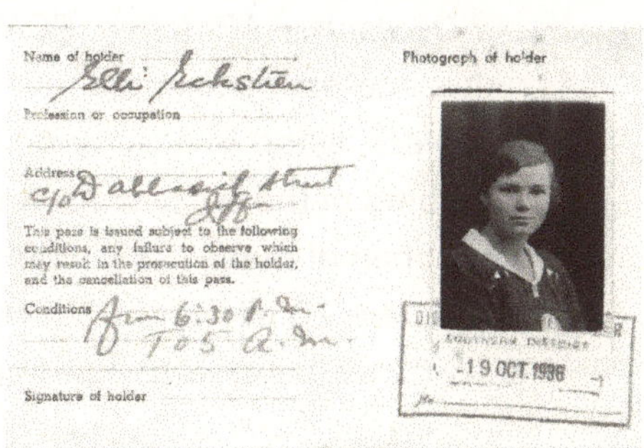

Name of holder

Profession or occupation

Address

This pass is issued subject to the following conditions, any failure to observe which may result in the prosecution of the holder, and the cancellation of this pass.

Conditions

Signature of holder

Photograph of holder

19 OCT. 1936

Elli Trefz curfew pass

Nazi Palestine

Undoubtedly, the *National Sozialistische Deutsche Arbeiter Partei* (NSDAP) had a foothold among some Templers in Palestine in the 1930s. How strong and widespread it was, is disputed. The Nazis deliberately structured community activities and groups around their ideology. This was the case in Germany as well as in other places where there were German communities, such as Palestine. Soon there were groups for women, professionals, sports and young people amongst others; all pushing the party line. This structure may have also appealed to some Templers as they had always organised their communities around faith, hard work, physical fitness/sport and community life since their earliest days.

There are lists of Nazi party members from the early 1930s floating round the internet, but, it's hard to know how accurate these are. Apart from a few well-known Nazi leaders, I have no idea which Templers were party members or 'fellow travellers' and which were not. The Trefz siblings were at least fellow travellers and do appear on at least one list I have seen. My uncle Otto Trefz was a party member, who joined in the early 1930s and had a membership number. Ida and Elli were members of the League of German Maidens (*Bund der Deutschen Mädchen, BDM*). Karl was in the Hitler Youth.

It is interesting to note that there were 741 Germans, mostly Templers, listed in a book on Nazis in Palestine[91], either as members of the party or its youth or specialist organisations. About half of these (369) were young people aged under 25 years, and 20 per cent (138) were between 26 and 40 years. Sixty (12 percent) were aged between 41 and 60 years, and 7

91 This data is extrapolated from form the lists in Heidemarie Wawrzyn, Nazis in the Holy Land 1933-1948, De Gruyter, 2013, Appendix 2, Pages 150-199

or only one per cent were aged over 61 years. While this may not be completely accurate, it shows how successful the Nazis were in influencing impressionable children, teenagers and young adults. These youth organisations encouraged sport and physical activity as well as craft activities for the girls. While such activities might well have existed anyway, the Nazis used them as a vehicle for promoting of their beliefs.

There was a Nazi branch, as well as Hitler Youth and *BDM* groups in the Templer colonies. Certainly, most Templers were proud German patriots and very nationalistic. Hitler and the Nazi party was the German government of the day and therefore also their government and they would be loyal to it. Germany was also a very long way away from Palestine and only a very few Templers had been back and forth to Germany and had actual knowledge of the Nazi regime in action. I can see how Nazi youth groups were attractive for some young Templers, aged from 10 through to 20 something, than perhaps for their grandparents.

My aunt Ida Trefz was a member of the *BDM* in Jaffa. She went on a trip to Germany in 1937 with other young women from the group. There she met the Führer himself and he shook her hand. She thought this a real honour and retold the story, well into old age.

In 1938, all German and Austrian nationals were expected to vote in a referendum on the annexation *(Anschluß)* of Austria into the German Reich. The British Mandate authorities refused to allow the vote to be held on their territory so the German government organised buses to take people to the port of Haifa, where they boarded the US ship Milwaukee. The ship sailed into international waters where the vote was held.

My father, **Johann Konrad (Hans) Eckstein (1905-1974)** and his good friend and soon to be brother-in-law, Austrian national **Franz Xaver Messner (1904-1975)**, both voted on the Milwaulke. I don't know how either of them voted, but I suspect they voted ***for*** the 'Anschluß' as many southern Germans and Austrians considered themselves as coming from the same stock. My father was very worried that he wouldn't be allowed back into Palestine by the British, as his visa had long since expired and he had been illegally in the county for about five years. Somehow there was little checking of those disembarking the ship and he was allowed back into British Mandate Palestine.

Fritz Trefz returns 'home'

In about 1920, my grandfather, Fritz Trefz, took his family back to Palestine and they settled in Jaffa. They rented an apartment above Buchhalter's mill, just outside the city of Jaffa. It was near the old bazaar on the edge of the old city and about 10 minutes' walk from the Jaffa Templer colony.

Friedrich Buchhalter (1885-1956) was a mechanic by trade and took over a steam-driven mill in Jaffa. Several other Templer families lived in the same street, including the Hahns, the Dosters and the Rohrers. Also, the Templer community owned the corner property.

The remaining four Trefz children, Wilhelm (Willy) Friedrich (1911-1919) having died in Germany, spent from early childhood to their early 20s growing up in British Mandate Palestine. It was a colonial lifestyle and as children and young adults, they generally led a carefree life.

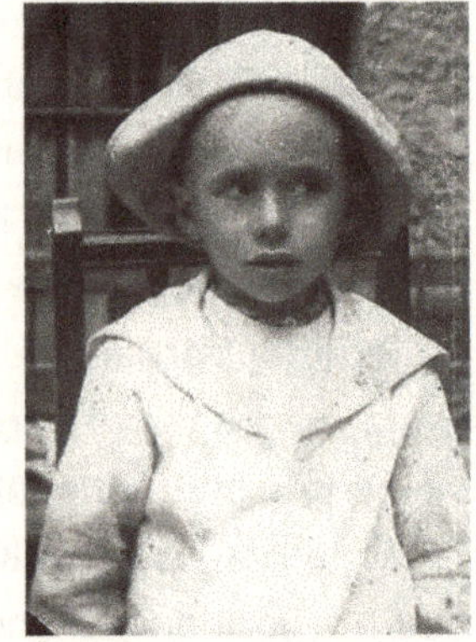
Willy Trefz (1911-1919)

Willy was always a sickly child,

The Trefz family home in Dabbasiehe Street (now Shim'on Ha'tsadik Street) in the 1930s.

Trefz house and street in 2012

Trefz house and street in 2016 – my grandfather Fritz would often sit on this balcony and watch the comings and goings in the street below

L-R: Ida Trefz, Anna Barbara Trefz nee Aichele, Karl Trefz on her knee, Otto Trefz, Elli Trefz and Fritz Trefz circa 1920

who caught bilharzia, a nasty tropical water-born parasite, in Palestine. He finally succumbed at the age of 8 years in 1919 in Neuweiler, Germany.

Otto was now the eldest and took on the role of leader of the Trefz clan, something that continued for the rest of his life. He became a tradesman like his father and worked in Australia as a fitter and turner. He married Anneliese Baldenhofer from Sarona in 10 February1939. They never had any children.

Hotel Jerusalem in Jaffa in 2016

Ida, being the oldest girl, took over her mother's role caring and keeping house for their father when Fritz' wife died of cancer in 1930.

Ida spent her time "*in Stellung*" at the Hotel Jerusalem (now the Hotel Drisco) in Jaffa, learning to cook in their kitchens.

In November 1938, she married Franz Xaver Messner (1904-1975), an Austrian from Golling near Salzburg, who had been

Franz Messner and Ida Trefz: Engagement

Ida and Franz Messner: Wedding

hanging around the Middle East for some years before he settled down with the Templers in Palestine. Shortly thereafter, just before the outbreak of WW2 in early 1939, they left for Golling, Franz's home village in Austria, near Salzburg. With the outbreak of war, there was no going back and Franz was conscripted into the German army.

Kaiserwerther Diakonissen Hospital in Jerusalem 2012

My mother, Elli took her mother's death in 1930, when she was only 14, very badly and never really got over it. After finishing school at the Templer school in Sarona near Jaffa in 1932, she spent two years in Jerusalem at the *Kaiserwerther Diakonissen Hospital* '*in Stellung*'. She worked in the office and also learnt how to cook in the hospital kitchens. Afterwards, she returned to the family home in Jaffa.

At 19, Elli became engaged to my father Johann (Hans) Konrad Eckstein (1905-1974), and about a year later, in 1936, she married him in the Immanual church in the Jaffa colony.

Hans and Elli engagement portrait

My father was a sheet metal-worker and plumber from Augsburg in Germany, who arrived in Palestine in a folding kayak (*Faltboot*) in 1932. He was 11 years older than my mother.

Anne Eckstein at
Immanuel church 2012

Hans and Elli wedding 1936

They rented an apartment in the basement of the three-storey Breisch house in Walhalla for two years until they returned to Germany in 1938.

Eckstein apartment in Breisch
house in 2012

Breisch house in Walhalla 2012

Karl, the youngest of the Trefz children, was only two years old when the family returned to Palestine after WW1. He was the classic *"Lausbub"*, naughty, cheeky and would regularly get himself into trouble. This continued throughout his whole life.

Karl Georg Trefz
(1918-2007)

He met Charlotte (Lotte) Emma Thomas from Friedrichroda in Thuringia (*Thüringen*) when he was at the School for Interpreters and Translaters in Berlin during WW2. They married first by proxy while he was still a prisoner of war in the United States. They married in person after the war in Augsburg in 1947 after he smuggled her out of the soviet zone; but that is another story.

Charlotte Emma Thomas (1920-2018)

Down the Danube in a Kayak

The German people suffered greatly during the Weimar republic and then the Great Depression. A Litre of milk rose in price from 20 Pfennigs in 1914 before WW1 to 6-9 million Marks in October 1923[92]. My father remembered being paid at lunchtime every day and running to the shops to buy bread before hyperinflation made the money worthless and the cost of a loaf of bread had doubled or tripled. In fact, when new notes couldn't be printed fast enough to keep up with rising inflation, authorities used a rubber stamp to print the new value on the old notes.

In the autumn of 1931, he and his friend Schütze[93] built a folding two-man kayak '*Faltboot*' and set off down the Danube River. My grandmother, Ottilie Clothilde nee Kunstmann (1880-1931), had recently died from Type 2 diabetes, when my father decided to leave to see the world on the trip of a lifetime. They

---

92 Article by Dr Cornelia Kirchner-Feyerabend: *Rosstaler Lebensbilder, Bürgermeister Hans Eckstein *8.4.1885, ▯28.2.1945*, in Rosstaler Heimatsblaetter No. 57, 2021, P. 9

93 My father's friend and travelling companion, Schütze's first name is no longer known.

Hans Eckstein (Right) and Schütze (with the oar) in front of the two-man kajak.

may have started their journey in Augsburg as the Lech River, which flows through the city, is a tributary of the Danube. The Lech joins the Danube near Marxheim, a distance of about 45 km. They may also have begun their journey further down the Danube at Passau or Regensburg, about another 100 km away as mentioned in my father's notebook about the trip.

Over many months, they made their way down the Danube, through Passau; Linz and Vienna in Austria; Bratislava in Slovenia; Budapest in Hungary; Belgrade in Serbia; and through Romania, finally reaching the Black Sea at the delta. They continued along the coast eventually reaching the Bosporus and Constantinople (Istanbul), where they met a German woman and stayed a while.

They continued into the Sea of Marmara and through to the Aegean Sea, and finally into the Mediterranean, where they continued paddling their kayak along the Turkish, Syrian, Lebanese (at Beirut) and Palestinian coasts, working here and there until, eventually, they landed on the beach at Jaffa.

Despite the language barriers, my father worked wherever he could get it, including the backbreaking work of digging wells for water. Instructions were transferred via several languages and no one was ever quite sure that all critical information had been correctly passed on. Somehow it all worked out; the wells were built, and no one was seriously hurt.

The *Südstrand* (south beach) at Jaffa was a popular hangout for young Templers. There was an old mansion, the *Villa Südstrand*, which was home to a German-speaking sporting club. Most Templers were good swimmers, living close to the beach and in the warm Mediterranean climate. One day, when a group of young Templers, I think it may even have included my uncle Otto Trefz, were enjoying the beach playing football (soccer) on the sand, two men in a small boat emerged from the sea and landed on the beach in Jaffa.

To the surprise of the locals and the visitors alike, they all spoke German! The two German travellers with their two-man kayak on the beach at the *Südstrand* were immediately surrounded by an astonished bunch of locals. "*Ja, wo kommt denn ihr her?*" (Where have you come from?), the locals wanted to know. "*Und was tut denn ihr hier?*" (And what are you doing here?), my father wanted to know. After exchange of mutual explanations, the two travellers were taken back to the German colony, fed and helped to find accommodation.

My father's friend Schütze caught malaria somewhere along the way and when he didn't recover, the German doctors in Jerusalem advised him to return to Germany. This left my father alone with a two-man kayak and unable to continue on as planned: down the Nile and into Africa and then on a steamship to the Americas. My father stayed on in Palestine for almost another seven years, marrying my mother in 1936.

He also found work among the Templers, including in the workshop of the Hahn brothers in Jaffa. The Hahn's lived in the same street as the Trefz family. That and through the

Templer sporting and social activities is probably how he met my mother.

My father became part of life in the Jaffa German speaking community, took part in social and sporting activities, and made friends among the Templers and other German speakers there. One of these was an Austrian named Franz Messner, who had been bumming his way around the Middle East for some time.

My father and Franz Messner became firm friends, despite a less than auspicious first meeting. They met in a tavern one night, where Franz got really very drunk.

The Reinhardt hotel in Ramleh in 2016.

My father offered to see him to his accommodation, which was supposedly at the Reinhart Hotel, in Ramla (*Ramleh*) about 16 kilometres from Jaffa, on the way to Jerusalem.

Halfway there, Franz said, no, no, he actually lived in Jaffa; so they turned back. Almost in Jaffa, he insisted that he really lived in *Ramleh*. This continued until almost the morning, when my father had had enough and he left Franz by the roadside to make his own way home (wherever that was), still completely drunk. Whether or if Franz actually got home that night, neither of them ever remembered.

Eventually, the two *"Deutschländer*[94]" (my father really resented that term) married the two Trefz sisters, Elli and Ida. Both couples married at the evangelische Kirche (protestant Immanuel church) in Jaffa; Elli and my father in 1936, and Ida and Franz in 1938.

---

94 *Deutschländer* was a term for outsiders, who came from Germany and not from original Templer stock.

A really bad idea

After their marriage, my parents lived in the ground floor apartment of the Breisch house in the Walhalla Templer colony. On 25 July 1938, my parents returned home to Germany. My mother had only lived in Germany for a few years as a young child but like most Templers, she considered it her home just as Palestine was also her home. They went to live in Augsburg in Bavaria, where my father had grown up and his family still

My parents looking out the window at Treustrasse 6

lived. This proved to be perhaps the worst decision they ever made because a little over a year later, the War (WW2) broke out and they were unable to leave Germany for the duration.

On arriving in Augsburg, they lived with my grandfather Eckstein in Hans-Adlhochstrasse 7 before moving to their own apartment at Treustrasse 6, in Pfersee.

In 1940, my brother **Walter Albrecht Eckstein (1940-2009)** was born. He grew up in Augsburg during WW2 and its aftermath when times were really hard.

My mother knitted his winter clothes and my father made his toys, including a pedal car, a sled and a wheelbarrow and wooden rocking horse. My father was very good at making almost anything out of metal. Later he would also turned his hand to building and carpentry; building our house in Boronia as well as making the windows and most of the furniture.

During the war, my father worked in an aircraft factory (*Martin Schmittner Flugtechnische Werke*) in Augsburg. This was a protected industry for the war effort and he didn't have to go and fight. After the war, the worked at his trades again as well as undertaking studies towards his Master Tradesman Certificates, which then allowed him to open his own business.

Elli, Hans and Walter Eckstein in the early 1940s.

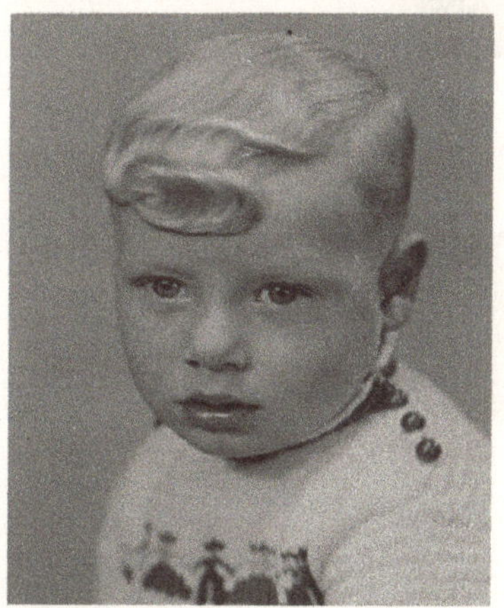

Walter Albrecht Eckstein (1940-2009)

Walter with his pedal-car

9. The Ecksteins from Roßtal

Johann Eckstein (1700-1755)** was my 6th great grandfather and was from *Gutsberg*. He married **Ursula Förtsch (1705-unknown)** from *Unterbüchlein*. Their son, my 5th great grandfather, also **Johann Eckstein (1730-1787)** was born and lived in *Roßtal*, near *Ansbach* in Frankonia (*Franken*) and was married three times:

- In 1755 at the age of 25 years he married Margaretha List (1729–1757). Margaretha died on the 4 Feb 1757 in childbirth with son Hans Eckstein (1757-1757);
- About a year later, he married his second wife, Anna Barbara Flurer (1723-1763). Anna Barbara had a daughter Margaretha Eckstein (1759-1832), but she died when Margaretha was only four years old;
- Finally, he married his third wife, **Catharina Wassner (1732-sometime after 1787)** in 1763. This third marriage produced eight children, including my 4th great grandfather.

My 4th great grandfather, **Johann Adam Eckstein (1766-1822)**, was the second child from the marriage with Catharina Wassner. He was a master stone mason (*Maurermeister*). Three children from that marriage died within a few weeks of their birth and there were several other sons but nothing is known about their lives. Johann Adam married **Margarethe Barbara Sitzmann (1762-1830)** in March of 1788 and in November of 1788 they had a son Heinrich, my 3rd great grandfather.

A soldier of Napoleon

Heinrich Eckstein (1788-1851)

Since 1792, Roβtal was part of Prussia. In 1806, the French occupied the area and gave it to the King of Bavaria. Bavaria was under the protection of Napoleon. Because of the alliance between Bavaria and France, many Roβtalers had to join Napoleon's armies. Napoleon gathered up soldiers for his armies as they marched through Europe and conquered territory. Those that had fallen needed replacing.

My 3rd great grandfather **Heinrich Eckstein (1788-1851)** was a soldier in Napoleon's army in the war against Austria in about 1809[95]. Bavarian troops also took part in Napoleon's disastrous Russian campaign, but it is unlikely that Heinrich was among them. Fortunately, Heinrich survived the encounter with Napoleon and founded a dynasty which leads down to me today and beyond.

Heinrich Eckstein was a master stone mason like his father. He also became the mayor of Roβtal. In 1812, he married **Katharina Schötter (1789-1862)** and they had five children:

- Johann Michael (1809-1857), aged 48 years;
- Katharina Barbara (1810-1811), aged 3 months;
- **Matthias (1814-1889)**, aged 75 years and my 2nd great grandfather;
- Elisabetha (1818-1889), aged 71 years; and

95 *Markt Roβtal website: Zeittafel zur Geschichte Roβtals seit der ersten schriftlichen Erwähnung*, 1792, 1808, and 1806-1813

- Elisabeth Katharina (1824-1897), aged 73 years.

The first two children were born illegitimate but their birth was later legitimised through the marriage of their parents. This was not uncommon at the time as some couples could only marry once they had enough money and/or could afford a house.

Matthias' younger sister, Elisabetha (1818-1889), married Johann Heinrich Fischhaber (1808-1873) of Roßtal. The Fischhabers also have a very long history in this town. When I was there in 2012, Fischhaber descendants still operated a tavern (*Wirtshaus*) in Roßtal as the family has done for generations.

Another Fischhaber emigrated to Saginaw, Michigan in the United States, along with many other Roßtalers in the mid-19th century. There, they founded the settlement of *Frankenmuth* in 1845, where their Bavarian or more accurately Franconian heritage can still be seen today.

Matthias' other younger sister, Elisabeth Katharina (1824-1897), married Johann Michael Eckert and moved to Weinzierlein. They had four children.

Building Rosstal

My 2nd great grandfather, **Matthias Eckstein (1814-1889)** was also a master stonemason in Roßtal, like his father and grandfather before him. He was responsible for building the 1838 extension of the school (*Schulhaus*)[96]. There is a plaque on the outside wall on the

96 Markt Roßtal website: Heimatsbuch von1928: Adolf Rohn: Das Schulwesen

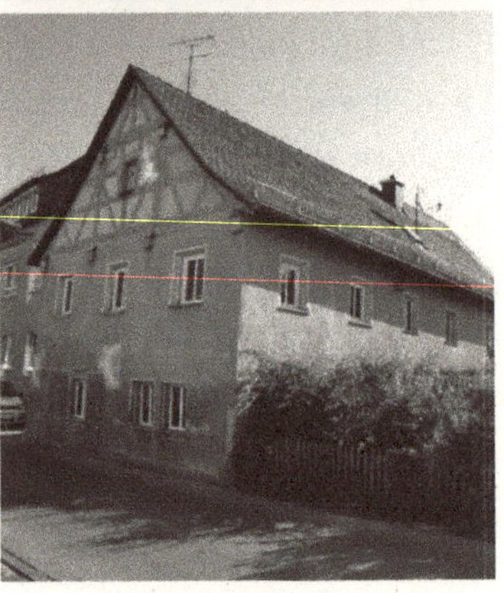

Matthias Eckstein's house in Roβtal in 2012.

western gable of the extension recognising his role. It says: M. E. (Matthias Eckstein) 1838 and shows two stonemason's tools: a hammer crossed with a double-ended pick. He was also a member of the Roβtal church council *(Kirchenrat)*.

In 1842, he married Anna Margaretha Burck (1818-1894) and had 10 children with her:

- **<u>Johann</u> Michael (1837-1909)**, aged 72 years and my great grandfather;
- Johann Konrad (1840-1890), aged 50 years;
- Katharina (1842-1914), aged 72 years;
- Michael (1844-1925), aged 80 years and mayor (*Bürgermeister*) of Roβtal;
- Johann Heinrich (1849-1929), aged 80 years;
- Margaretha (1851-1920), aged 69 years;
- Johann Adam (1853-1937), aged 84 years;
- Anna Katharina (1855-1856), aged about 1 year;
- Katharina (1856-1856); aged just over 1 month;
- Katharina (1858-unknown).

The first few children were born illegitimate although their birth was later legitimised through the marriage of the parents. Matthias lived with his large family in a house in Roβtal. It is now a historically protected building (*unter Denkmalschutz*).

My great grandfather, **<u>Johann</u> Michael Eckstein (1837–1909)**, was the oldest son of Matthias and Margaretha, but he was illegitimate, his parents not marrying until five years later. It was decided that he should be raised by his mother's elder brother and wife on the Burck farm at *Stöckach*, which is about 1km down the road. This couple had no children of their own and my great grandfather lived with them from quite a young age. He kept the Eckstein name and later inherited the farm, which is still in the Eckstein family to this day.

The Eckstein farm in Stöckach

A long line of Mayors

Matthias' third son, Michael (1844-1925) was the first son who was born legitimate. He was a master builder and also mayor (*Bürgermeister*) of Roßtal from 1912 to 1919[97]. When the church in *Buchschwabach* was largely rebuilt in 1882-1883, Michael was responsible for carrying out the building works[98].

The Burgschloß in 2012, bought by Matthias Eckstein for his son Michael and still in the family today.

Matthias bought the '*Burgschloss*'[99] (the 'castle', a rather stately *Fachwerk* or tudor style house) in 1870 and gave it to

97 Markt Roßtal website: Roßtaler Heimatsblätter 11 (1985), von Richard Preisel, Hans Eckstein

98 Markt Roßtal website: Heimatsbuch von 1928, von Adolf Rohn, Nachbarorte

99 Markt Roßtal website: Heimatsbuch von 1928, von Adolf Rohn: Das Schloß

his son Michael in 1878. He paid in cash! It's just down the road from the town hall and municipal offices on the highest point in Roßtal.

Michael married Rosina Gästner and they had four children:

- Leonhard (1879 1930), aged 52 years;
- Johann Georg (1881-1882), died in infancy aged 1 year and 8 months;
- Elisabetha (1883-1885), died in infancy aged 2 years and 8 months; and
- **Johann (Hans) Konrad (1885-1945)**, aged almost 60 years.

Michael also had a second family[100] from an extramarital relationship that predated his marriage to Rosina Gästner. Kunigunde Winkler lived near Michael's legitimate family with her and Michael's two daughters: Kunigunde (born 1875) and Anna Barbara Winkler (born 1873). The children from both families grew up together and played together as children.

Johann (Hans) Konrad (1885-1945) was also a master stone mason and builder, completing the qualification in 1919. He did his military service from 1905-1907 and later fought in the Great War. He inherited the *'Schloß'* from his father in 1908. Hans was very community minded. He was captain of the volunteer fire brigade in Roßtal for over 10 years. He was also a municipal councillor for five and a half years before being elected as mayor of Roßtal in December 1924

Hans Eckstein (1885-1945)

100 Article by Dr Cornelia Kirchner-Feyerabend: *Rosstaler Lebensbilder, Bürgermeister Hans Eckstein *8.4.1885, †28.2.1945*, in Rosstaler Heimatsblaetter No. 57, 2021, P. 3

for a five year period and re-elected for a further five years in 1929.

Hans' main achievements in office involved addressing major infrastructure projects which had been neglected for a hundred years or more. They included:

- building of a fire station;
- rebuilding the school, which was bursting with children from the growing population;
- piping fresh water throughout Roßtal and dealing with the town's waste water;
- redesign and reconstruction of the local roads; and
- establishing a dedicated building for a town hall and municipal offices so that the records and files would not need to be moved every time the mayor changed. (Until then, the elected mayor had to provide the meeting room for council meetings and storage for the council records and files. This could severely limit the choice of mayor!)

Hans Eckstein was politically nonaligned and just interested in serving the community. He was removed from his post in 1933 when the Nazi regime came to power because he refused to tow the party line. Seven weeks before the end of the war in 1945, he was shot and killed in his car by a low flying allied aircraft at the *Weinzierlein Berg* (more likely a smallish hill rather than a mountain!) on his way to the Fürth district office *(Bezirksamt).*

Hans married Johanna Lohbauer in 1908 and they had five children:

- Anna Babette "Bärbel" (1909-1986), aged 75 years; who married Friedrich Winkler and had seven children with him;
- Johann Leonhard (1911-1911), died in infancy aged six months;

- Johann Georg (1912-1944), aged 32 years, who was killed in Russia in WW2;
- Johann Leonhard (1918-1919); died in infancy aged 10 months: and
- **Hermine (Herta) (1927-2013)**, aged 86 years.

Hans also took care of his brother Leonhard's only daughter Johanna Luise Gertrud "Hanna" (born 1931) when she was only six years old[101]), after Hanna's mother died of cancer in 1937. Leonhard had died in 1930 of a heart condition, the year before Hanna was born.

Johann Völkl in 2012

Hans' youngest daughter Hermine (Herta) was born sometime after her brothers and sisters. She married Richard Völkl, who also became the mayor of Roβtal. And so the tradition continued...

Richard's son Johann Völkl was the mayor of Roβtal when I visited in 2012. He is a social democrat, so we had a lot in common. I am very grateful to him for a copy of his family tree and for connecting me to my Eckstein relatives in Stöckach. He has since stood down as mayor but remains involved with the historical society.

Back in Stöckach

In 1872, my great great grandfather, **Johann Michael Eckstein (1837-1909)** married Anna Margareta Weber (1844-1898) from Weiler near Rohr and they had the six children:

---

101 Ibid P. 10

- Johann Eckstein (1873-1957), aged 84 years, whose descendants still live and work on the family farm in Stöckach;
- **Johann <u>Konrad</u> Eckstein (1876-1956)**, aged 80 years and my grandfather who moved to Augsburg where, in due course, he became the chief postal inspector;
- Triplets (born 1878), two of whom were stillborn and the third, Johann Adam, died the next day; and
- Albrecht (born 1879), who moved to Vockenroth, married and had two daughters there.

Johann and Regina Eckstein with granddaughter Bärbel, about 1952

My grandfather's older brother, Johann Eckstein (1873–1957) inherited the family farm in Stöckach. He fell in love with the milkmaid, Kunigunde Weiss from Zirndorf, who was working on the farm. She got pregnant but they were not allowed to marry because she was just a farm hand and he was the son of the owner. The baby, Anna Magdalena Weiss was born in 1895.

Elise Eckstein
(1910 1991

My great uncle eventually married the more appropriate Regina Staubitzer (1873-1962) from the Christenmühle (christian mill) near Rohr in 1902 and they had four children:

- A stillborn boy, born in 1902;
- Katharina (Käthe) (1904-late 1930s);
- Johann (1906-1981), aged 75 years; and
- Elisabeth (Elise) (1910-about 1991), who moved to Nuremburg (Nürnberg).

Käthe Eckstein married Michael Wagner (1896-unknown) in 1926. They ran a tavern and had three children: Luise, Hans and Betty. When Käthe fell pregnant again for the fourth time, Michael insisted that she have an abortion as they couldn't afford another mouth to feed. Of course, abortion was and still is illegal in Germany, so she did not get proper medical care and died in the late 1930s from blood loss from the botched procedure. Michael was sent to prison for procuring an abortion. After his release, Michael married again and his new wife, Sophie, raised the three children.

Johann Eckstein (1906-1957), as the oldest son, inherited the family farm. He married Maria Ulrich (1910-1963) in 1938 and they had three children: Hans, Margarete (Marga) and Bärbel. They each married and have raised a tribe of children and grandchildren,

Johann (1906¬1957) and Maria Eckstein's wedding in 1938

Hans inherited the family farm in Stöckach, and until sometime before 2012 when I visited), continued to work the farm. His wife Gretel passed away suddenly in 2017. His oldest son, Helmut, is a career fireman, married with two sons. His daughter, Karin, is married with three sons. His youngest son, Klaus, is now the farmer on the Eckstein farm in Stöckach and his family also live at the farmhouse. It is, of course, a European farm, with cows, pigs, and chickens. They also have a few fields for hay and some grains, such as wheat and canola. There is a garden to grow vegetables and some fruit trees. Klaus has two sons and a daughter. He is also a local government councillor for Roßtal.

The Move to Augsburg

My grandfather, **Johann <u>Konrad</u> Eckstein (1876-1956)** was a second son and therefore not going to inherit the family farm. He was quite smart though and so it was decided he should go to Augsburg, where he could make his way in an administrative or clerical position. He joined the postal service as a lowly clerk and eventually worked his way up to *Oberpostinspektor* (chief inspector).

In 1903, my grandfather married **Ottilie Clottilde Kunstmann (1880–1931)**, the daughter of Heinrich Julius Kunstmann (1842–1892), an engineer with the German railways. Ottilie was born in Ingolstadt where her father was the departmental engineer (*Abteilungsinenieur*). Later he was posted to Augsburg and eventually promoted to district engineer (*Bezirksingenieur*).

In Augsburg, Konrad and Ottilie lived in several rented apartments but in time owned their own house.

Konrad and Ottilie Eckstein's house at Hans-Adelhoch-strasse 7 in Augsburg

By WW1, they lived at Hans-Adelhochstrasse 7 where they stayed for the rest of their lives.

Konrad and Ottilie had three surviving children:

- my father, **Johann (Hans) Konrad Eckstein** (1905-1974), aged 69 years;
- Albrecht Eckstein (1907-1982), aged 75 years, named after his uncle in *Vockenroth*; and
- Elisabeth (Liesl) Eckstein (1917-1982), aged 64 years.(I believe there may have been two more pregnancies between 1907 and 1917 but the babies did not survive.)

Hans and Albrecht Eckstein as children about 1910

Hans, a plumber (*Installiteur*) and sheet metal worker *(Spengler)* travelled the world and finally settled in Australia; Albrecht, a cabinet maker *(Schreiner)* married and stayed in Augsburg; and Liesl married a public servant *(Beamte*) and moved to Munich.

Ottilie died of Type 2 Diabetes at the age of 51 years. She was one of the early diabetics in Germany to be treated with the new wonder drug, insulin. In those days little was known about how much insulin to give someone and how often to give it. She died of the disease in 1931.Konrad lived to be over 80 years old but suffered from dementia in his later years. He needed care in a secure nursing home as he was prone to wander.

Konrad and Ottilie's three children had six children between them. My father, Hans, had two children, my brother Walter, who was born in Germany during the war, and me. I was born in Australia, after the family migrated in the mid-1950s. More about us later.

My uncle Albrecht had three children, two sons and a daughter. My cousins Richard and Alfred live in Augsburg with their families. Richard has a son and a daughter and Alfred a stepdaughter. Richard worked at the city's theatre on the production side, doing the electrics and making the scenery move. He later became an elected union official. Richard has four grandchildren. Alfred was a late comer to the family as was I. He also worked at the city theatre on the technical side after his military service. Gertrud married a public servant in Munich and was a bookkeeper. They have one daughter and two grandchildren.

My aunt Liesl lived outside Munich with her husband, a public servant in local government. They had one daughter, Ilse, who married late in life and has no children. She went to university and studied economics. She lives in Frankfurt and has had a long career working for the *Bundesbank* (Reserve Bank).

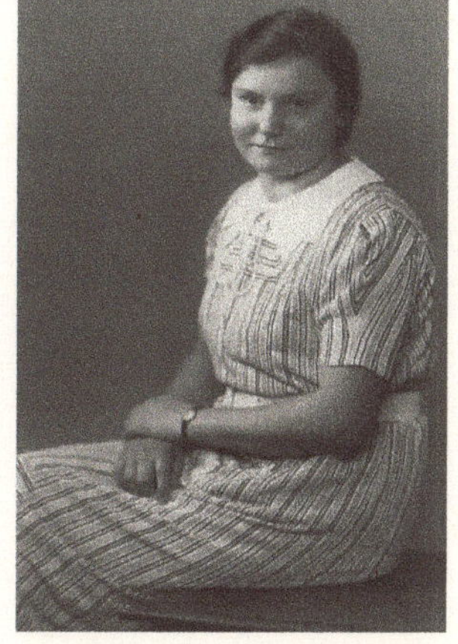

Liesl Eckstein about 1937

10. The Kunstmanns

My grandmother Ottilie Eckstein was born a Kunstmann. The Kunstmann family came from *Erlangen* near *Nürnberg* (Nuremberg), where the family owned and operated the university printery for several generations. Although they started as tradesmen, as printers and typesetters, eventually they came to own the business. As result, the family mixed with wealthy and well-educated people, students and academics. Also, through marriage into the Pfeiffer family and through them the (von) Billings, the Kunstmanns moved into the more educated classes and had connections to the minor nobility. Through these relationships, the family was connected to the noble families of the *Reichsritter Steigerwald*, imperial knights[102], a part of the Fanconian (*Franken*) group of knights of the Holy Roman Empire.

Ministers and Theologians

The Kunstmann family includes pastors and ministers of religion, theologians, doctors of medicine, and engineers. Unlike my other ancestors who were farmers, woodcutters and tradesmen, the Kunstmanns were able to move up the German class structure. My 2nd great-grandfather, **Pfarrer Adolf Ernst Christoph Kunstmann**'s mother was **Juliane Pfeiffer**

102 Reichsritter were free nobles of the Holy Roman Empire, whose direct overlord was the Emperor. They have their origins in medieval feudal society and heraldry. They had estates and exercised judicial and police control over them. Over time, the title of 'Imperial Knight' became a title of nobility rather than an occupation. They began to use the title '*Freiherr*' (Baron).

and she came from a long line of protestant ministers of religion and theologians going back to at least the mid-17th century. Her father was **August Friedrich Pfeiffer (1748-1819)**, a Professor of oriental languages at the University of Erlangen and *Hochfürstlicher Hofrat zu Brandenburg* (Councillor to the Prince of Brandenburg). Her grandfather, **Joachim Ehrenfried Pfeiffer (1709-1787)**, was a protestant theologian. In 1743, he became Doctor and Professor of Theology at the University of Erlangen. Joachim's wife, Sabina Dorothea von Billing, was the daughter of a protestant minister in Trautskirchen[103] and her family also had links to the nobility through the *Reichsritter* (imperial knights) *Steigerwald.*

There is also a distant family connection through the Kunstmanns to Friedrich Nietzsche (1844-1900), the famous 19th century German philosopher. I am also distantly related to the famous German writer, poet, playwright and novelist, Johann Wolfgang von Goethe (28 August 1749-22 March 1832), through his mother.

Dr Theology, August Pfeiffer (1640-1698)

Juliane's great grandfather, **Johann Ehrenfred Pfeiffer (1677-1713)** was Pastor in *Güstrow* and his father was **August Pfeiffer (1640-1698)**, a well-known German theologian. August Pfeifer was born in *Lauenberg*, the son of tax collector Philipp Pfeiffer and his wife, Maria Schneider. He studied at Hamburg and Wittenberg. In 1671, he took

103 The families of protestant ministers often intermarried with one another.

up a post as Pastor at the *Herzogtum* (duchy) of Oels and then at *Stroppen* near *Breslau* in Silesia (now in Poland). In 1675, Pfeiffer returned to Saxony, where he was the Pastor at *Meißen* and later became arch deacon in *Leipzig*. In 1684, he became Professor of oriental languages and then Doctor of Theology at the University of *Lübeck*.

My great grandfather **Heinrich Julius Kunstmann (1842-1892)** was the second and oldest surviving son of fourteen children of ***Pfarrer* Adolf Ernst Christof Kunstmann (1806-1876)**. Adolf Ernst Christof was born in *Erlangen* near *Nürnberg* and studied theology at the university there where the Kunstmann family owned and operated the university printery. He became a protestant pastor and was posted to *Burggrub* and later to *Mitwitz* in *Oberfranken* (Upper Franconia) near *Kronach* and close to the border with the state of *Thüringen* (Thuringia).

Memorial gravestone for Pastor Adolf Ernst Kunstman at the Jakobskirche in Mitwitz

Adolf married a local girl, Elisabetha Keßel (1819-1889) from Burggrub in 1839, after being posted there in 1834. In 1845, he was promoted to pastor at the larger church in nearby Mitwitz. He was the pastor at Mitwitz for over 30 years until 1976. There is a memorial gravestone on the exterior north wall of the *Jakobskirche* (Jacob's church) in *Mitwitz* to commemorate their much-loved Pastor Kunstmann and his wife. The inscription[104] on the top two stones reads as follows:

104 The inscription was given to Jürgen Herrmann from Nürnberg by Friedrich Bürger, local historinan in Mitwitz in 2018. It is presumed that the eldest son, my great grandfather. Heinrich Julius Kunstmann arranged for this stone memorial.

Hier ruht in Frieden (Here rests in peace)
Adolf Ernst Kunstmann
Kgl. (Königlicher) Pfarrer dahier (king's pastor here)
geb. Erlangen 16. Aug 1806 (born Erlangen)
gest.zu Mitwitz 22. Juni 1876 (died Mitwiz)

* * *

Elise Kunstmann
Pfarrersgattin (pastor's wife)
geb. Zu Burggrub 16. Okt 1819
gest zu Burggrub 10. Apr 1889

Gedenkt an eure Lehrer, die euch das Wort Gottes gesagt haben; Welcher Ende schaut an und folget ihrem Glauben nach. (Hebrews, 13,7)

(Remember your teachers, those who spoke to you the word of God.
Consider the outcome of their way of life, and imitate their faith.)

Adolf and Elisabetha Kunstmann had 14 children together, 10 boys and four girls:

- Karl Heinrich Adolf Julius Kunstmann (16 Jun 1840-22 Sept 1840); aged 3 months;
- **Heinrich Julius Kunstmann** (27 Feb 1842-9 Aug 1892), aged almost 50.5 years and my great grandfather;
- Karl August Kunstmann (14 Mar 1843-unknown);
- Henriette Therese Elise Kunstmann (9 Jan 1845-unknown);
- Gustav Adolf Kunstmann (23 Jan 1847-31 Dec 1911); aged almost 65 years;
- Emilie Kunstmann (13 Sep1848-7 Nov 1880); aged 32 years
- Maximillian (Max) Otto Julius (28 Jun 1850-unknown);
- Theodor Kunstmann (2 Sept 1851-5 Jan 1852); aged four months;

- Ernst Adolf Kunstmann (26 Jan 1853-3 Jul 1895); aged about 42.5 years
- Otto Eugen Kunstmann (28 May 1854-unknown);
- Gottlieb August Kunstmann (21 May 1856-unknown);
- Henriette Clottilde Julia Ottilie Kunstmann (6 Jun 1857-unknown);
- August Kunstmann (23 April 1860-unknown); and
- Johanna Bertha Kunstmann (5 Sep 1862-7 May 1876); aged almost 14 years.

All the surviving boys, who grew up to become teenagers, attended secondary schools at a time when most people were lucky to get any primary education at all. Some even attended university. As for the girls (children 4, 6, 12 and 14), they were expected to marry and only received minimal, education. There is also no information on what became of them. Several of Adolf Ernst Kunstmann's sons studied theology and became protestant ministers:

Very little is known about **Karl August Kunstmann (1843-unknown).** He went to the *Lateinschule* (Grammar School) at the *Königliche Kreislandwirtschafts- und Gewerbeschule zu Bayreuth* (Royal District Agricultural and Trade School in *Bayreuth*) between 1856-57 and 1862-63 when he was about 13 to 20 years old. He studied theology and was a good student achieving marks of mostly 1s and 2[105].

Goldsmiths in Kaiserslautern

Gustav Adolf Kunstmann (1847-1911) (4th son / 5th child) was a goldsmith (*Goldarbeiter*) and moved to *Kaiserslautern*. This is quite a long way from where the Kunstmanns lived in Mitwitz but it was still part of State of Bavaria at the time. On 15 May

105 German school marks are on a five point scale with 1 being the highest mark achievable.

1875, he placed a notice in the local paper that he had moved his shop from *Schillerplatz* (Schiller Place) to a new location in *Eißenbahnstraße* (Station Street). The advertisement says that he has a large range of gold and silver products, glasses and optical goods, hand-held opera glasses, thermometers, barometers and Christofl wares available.

Gustav Adolf Kunstmann was married three times. First, he married Anna Maria Louise Jost in 1883. She died in 1886, within a few days of giving birth to her second child, Gustav Adolf. Her first child, Gustav, was born two years earlier in 1884 but only survived for two days. Gustav Adolf's second wife was Maria Elisabetha (Elise) Buckel. Elise was a widow and brought a son with her into the marriage in June 1887. Four months later, she had a son with Gustav Adolf, named Otto Heinrich on 23 October1887. Elise died in 1889. Gustav Adolf Kunstmann married his third wife, Maria Johanna Anna Hiehle in November 1896 and in September 1897, they has a son, Erich Walter Adolph. Gustav Adolf died in Kaiserslautern in 1911, aged almost 65 years. Younger brothers, (8th son / 10th child), **Otto Eugen Kunstmann (1854-unknown)** and (9th son / 11th child) **Gottlieb August Kunstmann (1856-unknown)** followed Gustav Adolf to Kaiserslautern, also worked as goldsmiths and raised their families there.

The (5th son / 7th child **Maximillian (Max) Otto Julius Kunstmann (1850-unknown)** married Elisabeth (Lisette) Maria Baumgärtner and lived in Gunzenhausen near Rohr in Bavaria. They had four children: **Friedrich Julius, Elise Emilie, Gustav Adolf, and Otto**.

Ernst Adolf Kunstmann Junior (1853-1895) (7th son / 9th child) was a protestant pastor like his father and married Rosalie Sophie Faber. He served briefly as a Vikar in Straubing and later as pastor at Hain and Küps. He died from a fall when walking and climbing in the mountains, aged about 42.5 years. His son, **Theodor Adolf Ernst Georg (1878-unknown)** was a medical doctor in WW1. Theodor had two children: a son, **Hellmut Adolf Theodor Hans (1908–1979)**, also a doctor like his father, and a daughter, **Gudrun (1917–1994)**, who became a quite well-known sculptor.

An Engineer with the Bundesbahn

Heinrich Julius Kunstmann (1842-1892) was my great grandfather and grew up as the oldest son in the family; his older brother having died as an infant. Heinrich married my grandmother, Walburga Schuster (1843-1906) from Nassenfels, sometime before 1868, when their eldest son, Heinrich, was born. They had at least four children and possibly another two more, as yet to be found.

He attended the *Lateinschule* at the *Königliche Kreislandwirtschafts- und Gewerbeschule zu Bayreuth* from 1856-57 to 1858-59 when he was about 14 to 17 years. He was obviously a good student as he achieved mostly 1s and 2s. In 1869-70, he was studying to be an engineer at the *Polytechnische Schule zu München* (Munich Polytechnic), where he had received a scholarship.

Heinrich was an engineer with the German railways and was apparently influential in building the railway line from Würzburg to Gmünden. He was posted to Ingolstadt as a departmental engineer (*Abteilungsingenieur*) by the German railways. It was here that my grandmother was born in 1880 and a year later, her brother August in 1881.

In July 1886, Heinrich was transferred to the same level of position in Augsburg. Presumably, there were greater prospects for future promotion here, so the family moved. In 1888, he was still *Abteilingsingenieur* but by 1890 he has become the plant engineer (*Betriebsingenieur*) and in October 1891 he was promoted to district engineer (*Bezirksingenieur*). In 1892, at almost 50 and a half years he died in Augsburg.

Pfarrer Heinrich Kunstmann (1868-1926), my grandmother's older brother, was born in Nassenfels. He was a protestant pastor like his grandfather and uncles. He married Franziska (Frieda) Wilhelmine Frank and they had three children: Heinrich Carl, Frieda and Maria. He was the pastor at *Kirchfarrnbach* when his own son Heinrich Carl was born in 1900. Later he also ministered at the protestant churches at *Mainbernheim* and *Albertshofen*.

Uralt (Forever) *Nazi*

Heinrich Carl Kunstmann (1900-1964) was a German soldier in 1918 at the end of the Great War when boys and old men were being conscripted to fight in a war already long since lost. From 1919 to 1924, he studied medicine and graduated from the University of *Würzburg* in 1927 as a medical doctor (*Doktor der Medizin*). For a time, he worked at the University of *Heidelberg* Medical Clinic and became an Honorary Professor there in 1934. From 1934 to 1939, he was the medical director of the *Pforzheim* city hospital in *Württemberg*.

Heinrich was an early adopter of Hitler's ideology and became a member of the Nazi party in 1930. In 1939, he moved to *Hamburg* to take over the leadership of the *Gerhard-Wagner-Krankenhaus* (hospital) in *Hamburg-Friedrichsberg*, where he set up a centre for natural therapies. *Hamburg* was in the British sector after the war, and Heinrich Carl was interned for a time but his beliefs had not changed – he was unbroken, totally versed in the bible and anti-Semitic[106]. He became one of the most prominent extreme right wing politicians of the post-war period, being a member of the *Deutsche Reichspartei* (German Empire Party), who unsuccessfully contested a number of elections and then founded the *Deutsche Freiheitspartei* (German Freedom Party) in 1962. He continued to practice natural medicine.

Heinrich Carl's son, **Heinrich (Heiner) Werner Kunstmann (1941-2019)**, also became a medical doctor like his father and was head of nuclear medicine at the *Bonifatius Hospital* near *Lingen an der Ems* for many years until he retired in 2015. He died a few years later in 2018. Heiner was a highly respected medical expert. He married twice: his first wife was Karin Weise and they had five daughters. Quite late in life he married for a second time his childhood sweetheart and 'au pair' carer during the WW2, Irma Schuster nee Schlobohm. She ran a guesthouse, the *Gasthof zum Kiekeberg* in the Harburger hills south of Hamburg and had long since had her own family and children. They married in 2000 and Irma died in 2013.

The Curse of Diabetes

My grandmother, **Ottilie Clotthilde Eckstein nee Kunstmann (1880-1931)** died relatively young at the age of 51 years in 1931. She had Type 2 Diabetes. She was treated with Insulin injections, not long after insulin had been discovered to be useful in lowering blood sugar levels but long before it was

---

106 Wikipaedia: Der NS-Filmemacher 'Fritz Hippler' charakterisierte Kunstmann später wie folgt: „Uraltnazi [...] Im Internierungslager sah ich ihn wieder, ungebrochen, bibelfest und judenfeindlich" (The Nazi filmmaker Fritz Hippler later characterized Kunstmann as follows: "Forever Nazi [...] I saw him again in the internment camp, unbroken, totally committed to the bible and anti-Semitic".

Burial and gravestone for Ottilie Clotthilde Eckstein nee Kunstmann in 1931 reads : Hier ruht in Gott unsere unvergessliche Gattin und Mutter, Frau Ottilie Eckstein, Postinspektorsgattin.

known how to decide what the correct dose should be and how often it should be taken. She may not have been the first Kunstmann to succumb to diabetes as both her parents died in middle age, but she is the first one I know about.

Diabetes continues to ravage Ottilie's descendants. Both my father and his sister Liesl suffered and died from the disease; my father at 69 years and Liesl at 64. That is two thirds of Ottilie's children. At the next generation, again two thirds of the cousins from her three children have or have died from diabetes. That is, four of the six cousins, including two from her one child who did not have diabetes.

Mostly, Type 2 Diabetes is first diagnosed later in life. All of us were diagnosed around the age of 50, except for one of my cousins, who had led a very active life walking and climbing mountains. My cousin Richard didn't get diabetes until he was 70 years old. So, it is possible to delay it but not to avoid it entirely. It's a very nasty disease that eventually destroys the major organs; heart, kidneys, eyesight, circulation.

Another son of my great grandfather Heinrich Julius Kunstmann was **Johann Georg Julius (1874-1926)**. He was born in *Enzendorf bei Hersbruck* in 1874. Presumably, the family moved there for a time. He married Luise Lisette Rösch (1877-1960) from Schwabach. They had three children: **Karoline, Emilie and Georg Heinrich**.

11. Going home and leaving home

Wartime Germany

WW2 in Germany, and especially its aftermath, was brutal. My parents spent the war years in Augsburg, where my father's family lived. My grandfather, Konrad Eckstein, was still alive, although his wife, Ottilie, had died in 1931. My uncle Albrecht lived there with his wife and children and my aunt Liesl was still at home at the beginning of the war before marrying a public servant in nearby Munich and moving there.

My mother had only spent a few years in Germany as a very young child and wanted to return there. Born in 1916 in Jaffa in the midst of the Great War, she spent an arduous journey as a baby, travelling overland with the family from Palestine back to the Black Forest where her mother's family lived. In about 1920, when my mother was about 4 years old, the family returned to Palestine as did other dispossessed Templer families. My mother and other Templers still considered themselves to be Germans, even though they also considered Palestine their home. My parents married in Jaffa in Palestine in 1936. After years of Arab-Jewish unrest in British Mandate Palestine and with increasing tensions brewing in Europe, they decided to return to Germany in 1938. This was clearly not the wisest decision they ever made!

In Augsburg, there was a significant industry to service the Nazi war machine, including the *Martin Schmittner Flugtechnische Werke* (Martin Schmittner aircraft factory). Luckily for the family, my father was not conscripted into the army because he was a skilled tradesman; he spent the war years working at the aircraft factory, a protected and essential industry for the war effort. He was very lucky in that he could stay at home with his family for the duration of the war. Nevertheless, Augsburg was still a dangerous place and the target of many allied bombings because of the nearby military facilities. Augsburg, including residential areas, were regularly bombed and people headed into their cellars to survive. The house where my parents lived in an apartment was bombed a number of times and my father would put the fires out while my mother and the baby Walter took shelter in the cellar with the other women and children.

Germans knew something of what had happened in their name under the Nazi regime, perhaps not everything, but something. When I was a child, my father would talk about how he never went to civil defence (i.e. military) training during the war. This training was held in villages and communities as well as by employers, especially by larger industries. It was held once a week and compulsory for all males.

My father wasn't very keen on this so he told his boss at the aircraft factory that he was attending training in his local community at exactly the same time as the training was being held in his workplace. He told his community the exact opposite and didn't go to either. The boss at the aircraft factory would often threaten him with being conscripted *(Ich lasse Sie einrücken!)* into the military until one day my father cheekily replied that he thought it was supposed to be a great honour to serve the *Führer* and the *Reich*. After that, the boss threatened to have him sent to a concentration camp (*Konzentrationslager*).

This was a really risky thing to do in Hitler's Germany and shows that concentration camps were known about in the general community and that they were places of punishment at the very least. I will never know how he got away with it, but I am so proud of the stand he took at great risk to himself and his family, and also given he had this very Jewish sounding family name: Eckstein. In 2003, I retold a brief version of this story in my inaugural speech to the Victorian Parliament[107].

As the war ground on, some people were becoming increasingly aware that something was very wrong with the dream that the Nazi regime had sold them. Early victories turned into defeats and casualty lists grew, especially after D-Day in the west and the defeat at Stalingrad in the east. Rumours about German atrocities and extermination camps also began to circulate:

> *When the concentration camps were discovered, the Allies hung pictures of the atrocities outside town halls and showed films. ...... recalled that all the Germans he spoke to guilelessly told him they'd known nothing about it. But they'd all had a friend or cousin at the front or in the hinterland who'd passed on this or that to them.*
>
> *A lot of Germans knew something. They'd hear something from some cousin or other, and suddenly a curtain would be drawn back before them—but because they didn't really believe it, the curtain would fall shut again. Who, after all, would probe into a truth as awful as that?*[108]

Many people also chose to ignore, deny and disbelieve, even when confronted with the truth. Some are still in denial, over 75 years later. Sometimes you still find them; in Germany,

---

107 See Appendix 1

108 Huber, Florian, *Promise me you'll shoot yourself: The mass suicide of ordinary Germans in 1945*, The Text Publishing Company, Melbourne, Australia, 2019, P. 246

here, anywhere. One of my aunts, very late in her life when she was well into her 90s said to me: "Look, we were all Nazis. That's just how it was."

The war was lost long before Hitler shot himself in the bunker in Berlin and the generals signed the unconditional surrender. When people were actually confronted with what the Nazi regime had done in their name, it was like a "*Kahlschlag*", "*Nullpunkt*", "*Stunde Null*" (clear felling, absolute zero, zero hour); a complete levelling of everything they had believed in and held dear as well as the physical destruction that was everywhere to be seen. In many places, especially some areas of the larger cities, not a stone was left standing.

There is often a feeling of emptiness after a brutal war or a serious calamity but this was different. After the Great War, the German people felt humiliated by the Treaty of Versailles, which required Germany to pay hefty monetary compensation and give up territories that had been considered German for generations. After WW2, people were completely shattered. It was like a rug had been pulled out from under the entire population. There were feelings of betrayal, disbelief and despair in equal measure as well as good dose of denial and self-delusion. The immediate post-war period even sparked a literary movement: "*Kahlschlag-literatur*", which tried to make sense of these conflicting feelings.

With the suicide of Hitler, the cult leader and some of his immediate disciples, there was an epidemic of suicides of ordinary Germans; men, women, children, whole families died.[109] It started in the far east of the German '*Reich*'; in the German territories of East Prussia, Pomerania, and Silesia, ahead of the advancing soviet army, and swept westward. Small towns as well as cities; even the capital Berlin, were affected. It also

109 Ibid.

occurred in the west of Germany, but nowhere near to the same degree.

In the east, there was already an intense fear of the coming of the Russians, raping women and girls, burning houses and farms, and murdering people as they advanced. This was partially fuelled by historic fear of the Russian hordes, by Nazi propaganda towards the end of the war, as well as by retaliation for similar atrocities committed by advancing German forces in the war on Russia from 1941. The atrocities committed on all sides during war may be a reason but never an excuse for what took place.

The mass suicides of hundreds, even thousands of people in some places were not only from fear of the Russians but also from disillusionment.[110] Many Germans could not accept that the Nazi atrocities were real, dismissing them as 'fake news' in today's lingo. Others were wracked with guilt about what had been done, and yet others could not conceive of a future for themselves or their families without National Socialism. So, methodically and calmly they took their own lives. Fathers shot their children and then their wives and themselves, individuals slashed their wrists and bled to death in the bath, whole families took poison, mothers tied their children to their own waists and drowned them and themselves in rivers and ponds, and countless bodies hung from trees, in cellars and from the rafters.

Even 15 or more years after the end of the war, my parents often would still talk about it, trying to make sense of their experiences: What was true and what was not. What the regime had really done. Were 6 million Jews really murdered in the concentration camps or was it really much less? However, the mass suicides were never mentioned, maybe because my parents were in the western zone, where it was far less

110 ibid

prevalent, and maybe because by that time the mass suicides had already been consigned to the realm of myth; a memory just too awful to bring back to life.

Although as a child, I didn't really understand much of these conversations it did leave me with feelings of guilt and shame for what had happened in Nazi Germany, even though it was long before I was born and I had had nothing to do with it. I took that guilt and shame with me well into adulthood.

Surviving the Peace

Living conditions in Germany after the war were abysmal, especially in the cities. Food shortages were commonplace and many townsfolk regularly walked or cycled into the countryside to barter their possessions away for a few potatoes or to simply beg for food. On farms, at least people still had food: milk, eggs, potatoes and maybe a few vegetables.

Many people were also homeless or living in partially bombed out or burned out buildings, even through bitterly cold winters. People had little or no money and couldn't afford to make repairs or even buy materials or pay for tradespeople. It took well into the 1950s for Germany to begin to recover from the war. Not until Konrad Adenauer became German Chancellor in 1949 and his post-1950 *Wirtschaftswunder* (economic miracle) was implemented, did the country begin to improve. This was about the time my parents decided to migrate to the other side of the world, and they and my brother left for Australia in 1953.

My father had a plumbing business after the war from about 1947 until the family left for Australia. He was both a master plumber and a master sheet metal worker, having taken the *Meisterprüfung* (master tradesman examination) in

Hans Eckstein's Worshop at Pfladergasse 4, Augsburg, photographed in 2012

both disciplines in 1947 and 1949 respectively. There was a lot of work for tradespeople after the war, making repairs and restoring damaged buildings. Unfortunately, people had no money to pay for this work, especially after the replacement of the *Reichsmark* with the *Deutschmark* in 1948 and the resulting devaluation of the currency. My father had a workshop in the city, down near the river Lech. My mother kept the books and collected payments from customers who were reluctant to pay up. She was very good at getting money from people who wouldn't pay. Nonetheless the business was closed down and they left for Australia in 1953.

My father's younger brother, Albrecht Eckstein, named after his uncle, was a cabinetmaker by trade. During the war, he fought in Russia and was a prisoner of war there. He married Crezentia (Centa) Stengl (1913-2002) and they had three children together: Richard, born in 1938; Gertrud in 1941; and later in 1952, Alfred. Centa ran a small shop and they lived in Augsburg.

Albrecht and Centa's wedding

Richard and Gertrud as children

Liesl and Emil's wedding

Ilse

His younger sister Liesl married Emil Weinsdörfer (1911-2005) from Essingen near Landau in the Pfalz region. They had one daughter, Ilse, born in 1941; and they lived in Ottobrunn in Munich *(München)*.

Internment in Tatura

My grandfather Fritz Trefz and his brother Wilhelm together with Wilhelm's family were interned in Palestine in 1939 and later transported to Tatura in north eastern Victoria in 1941 with over 500 other Templers. They were expelled from Palestine by the British without knowing where they were being sent. First, they were taken by bus to the railway at Lydda and then by train to Suez via Gaza. Each adult was allowed 40 kg of luggage and the children 30 kg each. The 36-hour train journey was hot, crowded and oppressive with no food and little water. The windows were ordered to remain closed but were later able to be opened a little. At Suez the Templers were transferred by ferries to the Queen Elizabeth, which was anchored far out in the Red Sea. The ship had been converted into a troop carrier. She sailed south east. People still had no idea what their final destination would be. On the ship were over 1000 prisoners of war as well as 1000 German and Italian internees.

At first, they thought that perhaps the ship was going to South Africa, but when the voyage went on and on, people realised that their destination was somewhere very, very far away. Eventually the ship docked in Freemantle and then later in Sydney, where they were transferred to a train to Rutherglen and then onto the internment camp at Tatura by bus. Not only had the Templers been sent to Australia, to the other side of the world, but for the foreseeable future, they would be living in the middle of nowhere, in flimsy Nissan huts through scorching Australian summers and freezing winters.

The Trefz and Scheerle families at Camp 3 in Tatura.

The Trefz family were all housed together with the Scheerle family in a Nissan hut in Camp 3 in Tatura until about 1946, when they were released from detention to Stockwell, South Australia.

Internment would not bring the Templers down. As they do everywhere they go, they organised themselves and re-established their community life in short order. There were rosters for kitchen duties and work details. Schooling continued with classes organised for the children as well as religious services and confirmation lessons. My mother's first cousin, Annemarie (Amei) Trefz taught a class at the Templer school in the camp. Social activities, plays, Christmas celebrations were also held at the camp.

Once Germany had lost the war, I believe that there were discussions among the Templer leadership about whether the Temple Society should be disbanded, since Germany had been defeated and Hitler was dead. How could they even go on? Fortunately, wiser heads in the community prevailed, and pointed out that the Templer community and beliefs had been around for a lot longer than Hitler and the NSDAP and that the beliefs and values of Christoph Hoffmann and others had stood generations of Templers in good stead long before the Nazis arrived on the scene.

Waltercolour of Fritz Trefz in the internment camp at Tatura in 1943

After the war, the German internees were given the choice of staying in Australia and making a life here or being repatriated to Germany. Many, including Wilhelm Trefz and his family and my grandfather Fritz decided to stay in Australia. In the 1950s, many families joined them in Australia rather than stay in war-torn Europe. Only about a third of the Templers in internment in Australia chose to return to Germany after the war. They returned to a physically and psychologically devastated country.

Some Templers who had decided to stay in Australia were sending care packages of food and coffee to friends and family in Germany even though they themselves had little or nothing. I found a number of receipts for care packages from retailer David Jones sent to relatives in Germany by my great uncle Wilhelm Trefz amongst his papers.

Franz, Helmut and Ida Messner about 1940

Helmut Messner's grave in Augsburg in 1940

12. New beginnings

Migration and Resettlement

When my parents decided to emigrate to Australia, they had also considered the possibility of going to the United States. My grandfather, Fritz Trefz had written to his cousin Emma Weaver Bird in New York asking her to advise them about prospects in America. In the end, they decided to resettle in Australia, mostly because my grandfather was already here and he was not very well and unlikely to be able to make the long journey to the US. My great uncle Wilhelm and his family were here too, having also been interned at Tatura during the war. And many other Templers were already in Australia or planned to resettle here.

In 1950, my mother's older brother, Otto Trefz and his wife had already migrated to Australia to join her family, the Baldenhofers, who were already here. In 1952, my mother's sister, Ida and her husband Franz Messner, also migrated from Austria with their two boys, Sigi and Eddie.

Templer communities were beginning to re-form in Australia, both from those who had been interned here during the war and had decided to stay, and from family members who had come to join them from war-torn Europe.

In 1939, Franz and Ida Messner returned to Golling near Salzburg in Austria, newly married and already pregnant with their first child. Helmut was born in May 1939 but only lived 13 and a half months. He caught tuberculosis from his uncle Anton (Toni) Messner in Austria, who caught it as a soldier at the front. Helmut died in Augsburg on a visit to my parents.

My mother always blamed herself for Helmut's death, but the more likely cause was a weak immune system from poor nutrition and a lack of medicines to treat the disease.

The Messners had two more children, both boys. Siegfried (Sigi) Franz Messner was born in 1941 and Edmund (Eddie) Otto Messner was born in 1944. Sigi and Eddie both grew up to marry and have three children each. They now also have a tribe of grandchildren.

Ida, Eddie, Franz and Sigi Messner about 1947

Karl Trefz left Jaffa in 1939 on the last ship to Germany before the outbreak of WW2 to serve in the army. He fought on the eastern front, before being sent to train as an interpreter and translator in Berlin. It had become known that he had skills in English and Arabic from his time in Palestine. In Berlin, he met Charlotte (Lotte) Thomas, who was working there in a clerical job. After his training, he was attached to Rommel's Africa Corp but he was soon captured by the American forces and sent to the United States as a prisoner of war.

Once he returned to Germany after being released from

captivity, he lived with my parents in Augsburg. Karl then set about finding his bride Lotte and marrying her properly[111]. She had returned to Friedrichroda in Thuringia, where her family lived on a farm.

Thuringia was in the soviet / Russian zone and many years of separation from her family followed for Lotte because of the Cold War. Packages would not arrive at all or were opened and the contents looted. Letters were routinely opened and censored by the East German authorities. It was not until the mid-1980s, not long before the fall of the Berlin Wall, that Karl and Lotte were able to travel back to West Germany, including making a short visit to Lotte's remaining family in the former German Democratic Republic.

Lotte, Karl and Gisela Trefz, about 1950

As the crow flies, Frierichroda was not all that far from Augsburg in Bavaria, which was in the American zone. However, exit papers from the Russian zone were impossible to get and transport links were non-existent. So one dark night, Karl went to collect his bride Lotte and take her back to Augsburg. Lotte's father understandably did not want her to go but she wanted to make her future with Karl.

111 There had been a proxy marriage while Karl was a prisoner of war in the USA and Lotte was at home on the farm in Friedrichroda.

Lotte could only take one small suitcase, and they had to travel overland to the border; scrambling through the woods for the last part of the trip. They were not alone. Russian security guards were on the lookout for escapees and lots of people were also trying to get to the west using the same route.

Once across the border, they could get on a train and travel in relative comfort to Augsburg. They still had to worry about security checks because Lotte had no valid papers to be in the west. This also proved to be a problem when they tried to get legally married. Eventually, everything was sorted out and they lived with my parents in Augsburg.

Karl later found an apartment for them near my parents but it needed a fair bit of work as the building had been bombed during the war. Karl and Lotte's daughter Gisela was born in Augsburg in 1948. She married Gerhard Meyer, a lodger from Germany renting a room at their house in Boronia, but they later divorced. Gisela spent many years caring for her parents; firstly her father who lived to 89 years and then also for her mother, who lived to 98 an a half years old. Gisela has two married daughters and one grandchild.

In 1953, my parents and my brother Walter, together with my uncle, Karl Trefz and his wife Lotte and daughter Gisela, emigrated to Australia. They took the train from Augsburg to Genoa, where they boarded the ship 'Oceania' for the long ocean voyage south.

Other Germans and also some other Templers were on the ship as well; all looking to make a new life in Australia. This included Uli and Benno Asensdorfer, who also came from Jaffa.[112] The ship sailed from Genoa via Egypt, through

---

112 I thank Dr John Asensdorfer for this photo from his father's collection of my parents, Hans and Elli Eckstein, and his father Uli and uncle Benno Asenstorfer on the ship 'Oceania' on the voyage to Australia. It is probably the only photo I have where my mother actually looks happy.

My parents Hans and Elli on the ship 'Oceania' with Uli and Benno
Benno Asensdorfer

the Suez Canal and the Red Sea to Colombo and eventually on to Australia.

They had rough seas for a lot of the voyage. Everyone in the two families was terribly seasick, except my father who turned up promptly for every meal and wasn't seasick even once.

In the Middle East, my uncle Karl Trefz was in his element. Here is a piece of my aunt Lotte's diary of the voyage, when they reached the port of Aden:

On the 15th of March (1953) at 5.00 in the afternoon, we passed the exit to the Red Sea, travelled along the left coast, and arrived in Aden at 11.00 pm, where we stopped for six hours. We could go ashore and were taken to the harbour by motorboat. There was a glorious starry night and the brightly lit up port of Aden were a wonderful sight.

On shore, we both walked in a circle around each other for a bit before we decided to cross the city by car. It was a broken down, old wreck of a car and there were three black men in the front seat driving. I was terrified and I kept thinking about Gisela and Walter, who had stayed on the ship and were fast asleep. And these three guys were racing through the dark night with us both, and where were we going? ....I didn't feel at all comfortable with this situation and I whispered to Karl a few times asking him if he had a knife with him. Well, finally two of the guys got out along the way and my fears completely disappeared. After that, Karl chatted quite nicely in Arabic with the other one.

He told Karl about how he wanted to get married soon, but that he had to buy himself a wife first. The more he paid, the more beautiful she would be. Along the way, we saw policemen walking around wearing gaiters and with bare feet. In front of the houses were matrasses with sleeping black people on them. It was half past one in the morning after all. There were even half naked children, dusty and dirty, lying on the footpaths without blankets, sleeping like the dead. (It was a very sorry sight!) The driver then brought us back to the port in one piece and the voyage continued.

This was the first time Lotte had been anywhere else but in Germany, and it showed!

The ship docked in Freemantle before continuing on to Melbourne, docking at Station Pier, where all the migrant ships pulled up. When people had collected their belongings, Australian customs searched most of the trunks and luggage very thoroughly. The doonas *(Federbetten)* filled with feathers were immediately confiscated and burnt for fear of bringing disease into the country. Luckily, for some unknown reason, my parents' things were not searched and they kept their precious *Federbetten*, which kept us all warm during many a Melbourne winter.

Living in the 1950s

Australia in the early 1950s was no picnic but it was a long way from potential wars. My parents had also been told that there was plenty of work to be had, land was cheap so that ordinary people could afford their own house, and more or less that the streets were paved with gold! While that wasn't even remotely true, unskilled work was easy enough to find and basic English was usually enough to get by. Some Templers had English skills from their time in Palestine, but the language barrier proved a problem for many and there were few systems in place for having overseas qualifications recognised. Many had to take lower level jobs than what they were qualified for, my father included.

In Germany, my father was a master tradesman who had owned and run his own business. In Australia, he couldn't even pass the plumbing apprenticeship exam because of his lack of technical English. He was allowed to use a small German-English pocket dictionary during the exam but when he looked up the word 'thread', as in the thread of a screw, the dictionary gave him the translation for thread, as in sewing thread or cotton. He couldn't make sense of the question and so couldn't answer it. He passed all the practical tasks perfectly but not the written exam, so he gave up trying to become a qualified plumber in Australia. He then got work in his other trade as a sheet metalworker, which did not need a examinations or registration.

Post-WW2 immigration to Australia was in full swing in the 1950s and assimilation was the policy of the day: becoming 'like us' as quickly as possible, that is, like white Anglo-Australians, and forgetting everything else you know and where you came from. My parents talked about being asked to promise not to set up 'enclaves' before being allowed to come to this country. Multiculturalism had not been invented yet!

My mother's passport photo, 1953

I can remember my father being told, "We speak English here", when we were on the train into the city, speaking in German to each other when I was about 4 years old. He didn't understand and I had to explain it to him. He was humiliated and so was I.

Racist taunts were not uncommon either. I remember being called a germ and a Nazi when I was in primary school. Such experiences make migrant kids tough and make their communities turn inwards; living one kind of life in their homes and in their communities and another at school or at work or with other Australians. We change into different people when we go in or out of the garden gate. The Templers had lived in a German-speaking 'bubble' in Palestine, so living in another one in Australia was really no different.

My mother's 'bad nerves'

Not long after arriving in Australia, my mother was involuntarily committed to a mental institution for a serious mental illness, schizophrenia, in fact. I don't know exactly when that diagnosis was made, as I was only given that name many years later, in the late 1970s. Her behaviour was always erratic and unpredictable, even when medicated. She often became delusional: she firmly believed to have seen people who could not possibly be there (like family in Germany) and heard sounds and voices that did not exist (like cries for help, my brother's voice, when he was in Germany). My father had no experience of this and found it very difficult to deal with. At one point he considered leaving. Very early in her illness, my aunt Lotte said my father was ready to leave and abandon the family and she talked him out of it 'for the sake of the children': Walter and me.

Treatment options for mental illness in the 1950s were primitive to say the least (and you could say it's not that much better now). Electroconvulsive Shock Therapy (ECT) was being used routinely and was thought to be the magic cure. For my mother, it was not. Not only were treatments ineffective and she relapsed every six weeks or so as the ECT treatments wore off. It also totally scrambled her brain and her memory.

I am sure that the language barrier made both diagnosis and treatment difficult. At one point, a doctor suggested to my father that if she really wanted another child and had one, she might snap out of it; hence my arrival in 1955. Apparently, she was back to normal during the pregnancy but the symptoms returned as soon as I was born. In fact, she ran away from the hospital with me shortly after the birth. This was at a time when women were generally kept in hospital for a week or more after the birth of the child.

Regular hospitalisation and more shock treatments followed for months and then years. With the advent of antipsychotic drugs in the 1960s, the treatment changed. However, it was no more effective. The number and length of hospitalisations reduced, but the drugs had terrible side effects and turned her into a zombie for as long as she was taking them. Of course, my mother never accepted that she had a mental illness and would wean herself off the drugs at the earliest opportunity. Then the whole cycle would start over again.

I don't remember much about her illness during those early years as I was usually quickly whisked away. As a baby and then later as a small child, I was farmed out to relatives, particularly to my aunt Ida, at the first sign of aberrant or dangerous behaviour from my mother. Mind you, when you are very young, you don't know what's crazy and what isn't.

I do remember one incident when I was very small: I was on my father's shoulders and he was taking me into another room to my cot to go to sleep. For safety reasons, I slept in what was later to become the garage with my father and brother Walter while my mother slept in another room. I hit my head on the architrave of the door and started to cry. My mother came running over and hit my father over the head with a metal vase. It was the practical piece he had made to qualify for his *Meisterprüfung* (master tradesman qualification) in sheet metal work in Germany and he was so very proud of it. My mother was again taken away and I went to stay with my aunt Ida. The next day my father and my brother buried the broken vase under the house, for fear that the police would come and arrest my mother and take her to jail.

It was quite difficult growing up under these circumstances. I remember when I was five or six years old, coming home from doing the shopping with my father and brother to find every door and window in the house wide open and my mother sitting under the weeping willow tree in the backyard with the family bible in one hand and a large kitchen knife in the other. She was surrounded by half a dozen other knives. My brother quickly whisked me away to my aunt Ida's and my father got the doctor. My mother was again taken away to the mental hospital.

Eventually, I realised what was really wrong with her. I had always been told that she had 'bad nerves' and we all needed to be quiet around her so she didn't get upset. Of course, I was shielded from most of the really ugly stuff and mostly, I was too young to either understand or remember too much of it. Walter was a teenager. He saw and experienced all of the ugliness; much more than he ever should have. I believe he was deeply affected. When I was about 12, the penny finally dropped and I was very shocked and very angry. The relationship with my mother was never the same again.

My mother's illness was always called 'bad nerves' outside the family. It was shameful and not to be discussed with strangers. I hid the truth from all of my school friends for years and years. I was already living separate lives; one at home, another in the Templer community and yet another with my friends at school. Just one more secret to keep!

My father's passport photo, 1953

The stress on my father was enormous. He stood by us as a family despite my mother's peculiar thoughts and behaviour. My father had to always be on his guard, looking for signs of another breakdown coming on, making sure I was safe, and enabling me to grow up as normally as possible. I am sure it sent him to an early grave.

Building a home

When my parents arrived in Boronia in 1953, there was the railway station and very little else. As a very young child, I can remember the State Bank, a post office and a handful of shops: a baker, a butcher and a real estate agent. That was about all. It was like a tiny country town. Ringwood was the nearest town large enough for people to do their banking, shop for clothing and household goods and get tools and building materials.

Not long after my parents arrived in Australia, they were able to rent some rooms in the house of another Templer family, Johannes and Maria Klink and their children in Burke Road, Ferntree Gully. They were still living there when I was born in 1955. My father bought a block of land in Maryborough Road, Boronia on which to build the family home. It took my father and my brother Walter over four and a half years to build this house, working after school and after work every day until it got dark, and all holidays and every weekend.

Firstly they had to fell a lot of large gums and other trees on the block. Then concrete foundations for the cellar were poured. The cellar would later house the garage, the laundry, a small storeroom as well as storage for kindling, wood and briquettes for the stove. We lived in the cellar until the living areas of the house were finished and we were able to move in upstairs. This took until about 1958 or 1959.

When we lived in the cellar, we lived mainly in what would later become the laundry. There was a wood-heated copper for washing clothes and heating bathwater. My father had made the tin bath that we all used for bathing. We lived, bathed, washed clothes and cooked in what was later to become the laundry. There was a large table we used to sit around as well as an icebox to keep meat and dairy products cool and fresh.

Our finished family home in Maryborough Road, Boronia

I remember that the ice-man would come three times a week to bring the fresh ice.

My mother's cooking pots would bubble away around the edges of the copper or on the small wood-burning heater that was in the passageway to the garage. In the cold winters, we all huddled around the small wood-burning heater. In the hot summers, my mother cooked on a Primus, as they did in Palestine.

My mother slept by herself in what later became the storeroom. This was supposedly to spare her 'bad' nerves. The rest of us slept in what later became the garage, mainly for our own safety. The toilet was an out-house with spiders, down in the backyard which would be emptied by the night-man in the early hours of the morning.

Once the house was finished, we could move upstairs, where there were greater comforts and there was an inside toilet. An electric refrigerator was purchased and then an electric stove. We also cooked on a slow combustion stove, which heated the kitchen and provided hot water in winter. My father made most of the furniture as well as building the house itself; including a corner sofa (*Eckbank*), kitchen and other cupboards, a wardrobe and the living-room cabinet where the few treasured items were kept that had survived the war and the voyage to Australia.

My father had earlier made all the windows and window frames for the house from plans sent by my uncle Albrecht in Germany, who was a cabinet-maker. The windows in our house opened inwards as they do in Germany so that they could be cleaned from the inside. (This can be quite useful on a multi-storey house.) Inward opening windows were not available in 1950s Australia – I am not sure they are even now. Although he had never worked with wood before, my father was one of those people, who could turn his hand to anything.

My mother hardly ever left the house. Whether this was part of her mental illness or some other craziness, I'm not sure. In any case, for about 15 years she never left the family home, except for an occasional visit to the doctor or to see her sister Ida. My father did most of the weekly shopping on Friday nights after work or on Saturday mornings, if he wasn't working overtime.

In those days, a lot of goods and services were home delivered. When I was a small child, milk was delivered daily by the milkman with his horse and cart. Later the milkman progressed to driving small a tray truck. A baker's van also came and sold white bread and rolls, at first daily and later three times a week. Fresh vegetables were also available from the greengrocer's van that came twice a week.

Best of all, Fritz Kroh came every Thursday with his VW bus filled with European foods and treats. He sold cured meats, salamis and fresh sausages; rye breads and pumpernickel;

real cheeses that didn't taste like soap; and packets of Dr Oetker puddings, baking powder, vanilla sugar and other baking goods. At Easter, he had egg dyes to colour real hard-boiled easter eggs and at Christmas he sold red and white candles, candle holders, lametta, chocolate covered Christmas biscuits and gingerbreads.

Also, once every three or four months, my father would take half a day off work and go to the Victoria Market in the city to stock up on European foods, especially ones that would keep for a while, like salamis.

In the 1960s life changed, the population in the area exploded: housing estates sprang up everywhere, new schools were built, and a handful of shops grew into towns. The Boronia township grew with many more shops and even several supermarkets built. Then came a K-Mart and the Mall, where young people would hang out with the advent of late night shopping on Friday nights. Home services and shopping fell away over time. But they did allow my mother to function and run the household with almost never leaving the house. Even the butcher, Fritz Kroh, gave up his VW bus and moved his delicatessen business into a permanent shop in Boronia in the late 1960s.

* * *

My mother died in 1988. She spent the last eight years or so living alone in the house my father and brother had built. She used to say that my father built it for her, not for us as a family. She was discovered dead in her bed one Monday lunchtime after 'Meals-on-Wheels' staff called and couldn't get an answer from her. They called police, who broke in and found her dead.

13. Big brother Walter

When my brother Walter arrived in Australia, he repeated the last year of primary school because my parents thought it would allow him to learn English by re-learning familiar material in a new language. By the end of the year, he had mastered the language and was near the top of his class. The next year he went to Ferntree Gully Technical School, a boy's school for non-academic students, where he stayed for three years. He then did an apprenticeship as an electrician, and later did a number of classes at night school, including a course in refrigeration at Swinburne Technical School.

Walter was a fast learner and excelled at his studies. He really should have gone to a high school and then to university. He was certainly smart enough but Ferntree Gully Tech was the only secondary school nearby and my father wanted him to learn a trade.

After school, Walter had to help my father with building the family home, managing the household during my mother's mental illness, and looking after me. It was a big ask for a teenage boy. I don't remember my parents saying that he complained all that much but then my father wouldn't have allowed that anyway. In our house you accepted how things were and then just got on with it.

Paddling down the Murray River

In January 1960, Walter paddled with a group of Templer mates down the Murray River from Echuca to Swan Hill in a home-made two-man kayak. They took their boats and luggage on the train to Echuca and then back home from Swan Hill.

I well remember the home 'workshop' on our terrace where Walter's kayak was built. My father supervised the works based on the plans for his own boat which had taken him down the Danube those many years ago. My mother sewed the canvas top on her treadler sewing machine. (It was never any good for sewing fine fabrics after that!) The canvas was then stitched by hand to the rubber waterproof skin of the boat. The wooden frame could be taken apart for easier transport.

There was a whole tribe of young men working on this project. My cousin Sigi was there and so were several more young Templers, including Sigi's best friend Uli Höfer. They built another boat to row together. Rolf Imberger and Jörg Imberger shared the third boat and Hennig Imberger was the other paddler on Walter's boat.

After they arrived in Echuca, the boys went shopping for food and supplies and then assembled their kayaks on the river bank. Then they started rowing. Along the way, they passed a raft of high school students. They also ran into an Englishman in a homemade rowing boat with a sail. He was heading for the mouth of the Murray River. There was also the German kayaker whose boat they ran into and punctured a hole in his hull. They shared lots of adventures, including: a wild pig chase, shooting at ducks, and a sinking boat after hitting a snag. When they arrived in Swan Hill they were met by a bunch of locals and reporters. There was even a small article and a photo in the newspapers at the time.

Walter and his mates paddled down the Murray River long

before there was an annual race. In 1969, a 5-day race began along the mighty Murray River from Yarrawonga to Koondrook to raise funds for the Red Cross.

An overseas adventure

In 1963, Walter sailed for Germany, hoping to see Europe on a sort of 'Grand Tour'. Our cousin Sigi was going to join him about six months later and had already booked his passage. A broken heart from a failed romance led Sigi to cancel his plans.

Walter and I just before he left for overseas in 1963.

Walter worked through the winters while he travelled around during the summers. He stayed at youth hostels and slept on beaches, as did a lot of young people bumming around Europe at the time. Walter was also continuing the family tradition for travel and adventure. He did not return to live in Australia for another 20 years.

Travelling on an Australian passport at the height of the Cold War, Walter was able to travel in Eastern as well as Western Europe and being able to speak German didn't hurt either. It was particularly useful for travel in the German Democratic Republic (GDR), an opportunity not really open to ordinary West German citizens. Australia had not recognised the GDR at the time, so when the East German border guards gave him a hard time, he would refuse to deal with them, demanding that they go and get the Russians as Australia only recognised them.

The East German guards were not best pleased and neither were the Russians, who resented have to deal with such trivial matters and quickly sorted out their East Germans comrades.

Walter travelled by himself all over Eastern and Western Europe in the first few years after he arrived back in Germany. In 1966, in what was then Czechoslovakia, he met and later married Ingrid Sykora nee Gall, who had a six year old daughter, Leona (Loni). Her first husband had left her to skip the country and live in the West. It took some time after they married for Walter to get approval for them to leave the country, and later for Ingrid's parents to move to West Germany as well.

Walter and Ingrid lived in Nuremberg for almost 15 years. They travelled a lot and he even learnt to ski, even if somewhat badly. Although not qualified as an electrical engineer, he eventually got a good job, which paid quite well and Ingrid worked part-time. They had a comfortable life. There were work trips to Italy to commission projects.

After our father died in 1974, he came out to Australia for two months, helping me to sort out some of the legal matters. Three years later, I went overseas for the first time in my life and based myself with Walter in Nuremberg while I travelled around, got to know my father's family and eventually studied German linguistics at Trier University.

Walter, Ingrid and Loni's first Christmas

Walter and Ingrid were already building a house *Heligenstadt* in the Franconian Swiss region of Bavaria. There was even a castle on a hill overlooking the plot of land they were building on. Just like it was for my father, it was a weekend and holiday job and they worked on the house when they had the time and money to do the next part.

By the late 1970s, Walter's marriage to Ingrid was wearing thin. He had a good job AEG (*Allgemeine Elektrizitäts Gesellschaft*), and he was now commissioning power stations in several developing countries around the world, including in Iran during the fall of the Shah, Thailand and Korea. He wasn't really happy though, more like just treading water.

In Iran, Walter's health hit the wall. He had a major heart attack in the middle of the revolution against the Shah. He didn't get proper healthcare until he was back in Germany, as maintaining the electricity in hospitals wasn't really a priority during the revolution. He also hadn't looked after himself for a long time. He had smoked heavily since his late teens and drank heavily as well, with Black Label Johnny Waker whisky with Coke his preferred poison. He was a big bloke, like my father, and he regularly used a sauna as a weight loss tool. Even at 40, this was not a very wise thing to do!

In Korea, he met (and later married) Sunhi Kim. The next thing I know, he turns up in Australia one morning in mid-1980 and says he has met someone, he's going to get a divorce from Ingrid and then marry Sunhi. He is on his way back to Germany to tell Ingrid and sort it all out. A little boy named Tommy was born in 1982.

In 1983, Walter brought his new family back to Australia. The split with Ingrid was bitter. She hadn't seen it coming. He had to agree to pay her out so she could finish the house they had been building in Heiligenstadt as well as sign it over

Walter and Sunhi's wedding in Korea

to her, otherwise she would have dragged out the divorce.

Getting a well-paying job in Australia proved difficult as Walter had few recognised formal qualifications. Eventually, he was offered a job in the petrochemical industry in New Zealand and the family moved there. A few years later, they returned to Australia and settled down in a small house they bought in Ferntree Gully. The family now included Namie, Sunhi's eight year old daughter from her first marriage in Korea.

Walter learned to settle for less well paid jobs than he was used to in Germany. Sunhi eventually learned some English. The children went to local schools: Fairhills Primary School and Fairhills High School. Walter suffered from ill health for the rest of his life, including heart problems and diabetes. Although he gave up the cigarettes in his 40s, he kept drinking until he passed away in 2009 at 68 years from multiple organ failure. His son Tom, has grown into a beautiful adult with a wonderful family, including a daughter and a son.

14. Another child might snap her out of it

Growing up Templer

Growing up, we were loosely connected with the Boronia Templer community. My mother's sister and two brothers and their families all lived in the four or five streets around the Boronia Templer Hall in Wadi Street. It was the first community hall built in Australia by the Templers. It had a church bell in a bell-tower which rang for Sunday services and weddings. The Hall was also used for a range of other community events: German school classes, meetings, significant family celebrations like anniversaries and birthdays, sporting carnivals (tennis and 9-pin bowling) and whatever brought the community together.

The Hall was built entirely by community labour with the only possible only exception being my father. He refused to have anything to do with it until such time as he had built a house for his own family and put a roof over their heads. This led to a life-long rift with the Templers, and for the rest of his life, my father never once set foot in the Boronia Hall again. At family weddings, he would wait outside until the service was over.

I therefore grew up in and around the fringes of the Templer community. We actually lived a short walk from most of the Boronia community and my parents weren't financial members until I was much older. My mother considered herself a Templer whether she was financial or not, but as she hardly ever left the house, she never went to anything anyway. My father avoided most Templer functions and activities and was quite happy not to be living too close.

At my Aunt Ida's insistence, I was sent to Templer German school from Year 3 to Year 10, which I mostly enjoyed. I learnt to read and write in German from a lot of dedicated teachers, most of whom were not formally qualified as teachers either in Germany or in Australia. I very much appreciate that opportunity now as it allowed me to develop my first language to quite a high level. In the 1980s, after I qualified as a primary teacher, I spent 10 years teaching German at the Bayswater-Boronia Templer Community Language School.

At my mother's insistence, mostly because she thought she was going to die soon, just as her mother had done when she was 13, I was confirmed a Templer at the age of almost 13. I remember attending the lessons but none of the content. This was about the time I had started to question my religious beliefs. I never joined the Temple Society as an adult because I am not a believer in any faith.

I regularly go to the annual Templer Sommerfest picnic, where I can catch up with family and people I know and buy the odd German book for a gold coin donation. As a child, I attended two children's summer camps at Point Lonsdale, and as adult, in 2012 and 2016, I took part in two Templer trips to Israel to better understand the Templer experience in Palestine. I learnt a lot about the early Templers; where my parents and grandparents lived, and saw my great grandfather's grave in Jerusalem. I was very surprised by how much Templer history is preserved in Israel.

Going to school

On my first day at Boronia Primary School, I hardly understood anything that was going on. My English was really poor. Even though I had played with the neighbourhood children, I hadn't gone to Kindergarten. I remember, the teacher gave me a wax crayon and a large sheet of paper. I now realise that it was a chance for me to draw a picture but I hadn't understood what she had said as we spoke only German at home and there were hardly any neighbourhood children from whom to learn English. I thought she had wanted the crayon worn down so that's what I did and scribbled all over the paper. This was not really a great start to a career in education!

Determined not to smile

Another great impression I made on my Prep teacher was for drawing flags. The class was asked to draw a flag on small blackboards or slates where we did most of our writing and drawing. Slates could be used over and over again and were practically indestructible. The chalk was cheap and the children would clean the dusters. The class was asked to draw a flag on their slates and the teacher showed us how to draw the British Union Jack. Easy enough for even a Prep class, you say! Well, I had to go and ask the teacher whether I could draw a different flag. The Union Jack was too easy, I said. She hesitated but said that yes I could. Of the almost 60 children in my Prep class, all but one, me, drew the Union Jack. I drew the Soviet Union's hammer and sickle! This was not really the thing to do in 1961 when the Cold War was raging. Once the teacher realised what I had drawn, she quickly whisked it away from me and took it to show to the Head Teacher.

In my first year of school, I got every respiratory bug and childhood disease going around, including measles and mumps, so I was hardly ever there. Having not been at Kindergarten or been exposed to lots of other children before, I had no resistance to anything. After that year, I always did quite well at school, winning an academic prize at the end of primary school and I was always in the academic stream at secondary school.

My mother was committed again when I was in Year 1 and I was sent to live with my aunt Ida again. One day, I called my aunt Ida: 'Mum'. She was really angry with me and told me off in no uncertain terms. I knew she wasn't my mother even as I said it. I was actually just trying to acknowledge the important place she had in my life. I never did it again.

My later primary school years were largely enjoyable but uneventful. In year 2, I was transferred to the newly built Boronia West Primary School (PS), which was closer to my home. I did well at school; I had friends, who generally didn't live nearby; and if they did, we played at their houses, or outside in the garden, or down at the nearby creek. School was the normal world which I liked but tried to keep away from my crazy home. My father also had ways of keeping the craziness at bay. He would spend a lot of time tinkering in his workshop and on Sunday mornings, he would take me on long drives in the countryside, sometimes dropping in on my aunt Ida and my uncle Franz before going home to a late lunch.

After primary school, I went to Boronia High School, which was across the road from Boronia West PS. I enjoyed the academic focus, and learning a new language, French. I always did quite well. The first subject I ever failed was Maths in Year 11 and that was mostly because I needed get glasses to be able to read the little squiggles on the blackboard that year. I was sitting down the back of the room where all the 'cool' kids were.

First day at Boronia High School I 1968.

In my mid-teens, my mother had yet another serious mental breakdown which worsened over several years and finally she had to be involuntarily and forcibly committed again. She would spend her days wandering about the streets, telling people she had seen her son (who was in Germany) go into their houses. She wrote to Willy Brandt (Chancellor of Germany at the time) insisting he was her older brother Willy, who had died at the age of eight in 1919. She would visit other Templers in the area, telling them crazy stories and how badly she was being treated, none of which were true.

She had long since stopped taking her medication, because she believed there was nothing really wrong with her. This led to a lot of arguments all round, between my parents and with my mother. She could lash out verbally and sometimes physically if she didn't get her way. She was also trying to impose standards of behaviour on me from 1930s Templer Palestine in 1970s Australia. Naturally, I rebelled!

My father was also quite ill and nearly died from undetected internal bleeding after a car accident on one of those Sunday morning trips. One night, when I was due to visit my father in the hospital with my aunt and uncle, my mother locked me in and refused to let me go because it was already dark. My father told my aunt Ida and uncle Franz to get me out and I grabbed a few things and stayed with them for the next few months until my father recovered.

Now that I was living with my aunt and uncle, there had to be a certain amount of 'fessing up' at school. In my haste to leave, I had only grabbed a few essentials for school and my summer school uniform. A few weeks later, it was time to start wearing the winter uniform, which of course was at home with my mother. I couldn't go and get it because she was completely unpredictable and could have reacted violently. My aunt signed a note to the school (which I wrote for her) and which explained the bare essentials of the situation. I was off the hook for a while at least.

About a year after my father recovered, my mother completely lost it; locking herself in her room, smashing a window pane, and attacking my father with a pair of steel knitting needles. The family doctor was called but didn't turn up; the police arrived and finally got the doctor to come. An ambulance arrived and the police broke into her room. She was unceremonially pick up from her bed and carried to the ambulance, which took her off to the mental hospital. The next day my father and I met with her doctors and she finally got some treatment.

My teenage years were challenging. I had to take on adult responsibilities when I just wanted to be like everyone else. There were times when I just wanted to run away and I actually thought seriously about doing just that. Instinctively, I knew that the only way out of this mess was through education and into a good job that could provide me with a future. I learnt how to put my world into different boxes and keep them separate from each other.

After more than 45 years, I recently reconnected with some of my close high school friends. They had no idea, not even suspected, about my other life at home. They were shocked that they had not known at the time. They asked whether the school had known and provided any support. In those days, teachers and schools didn't get involved in anything that wasn't strictly education. I was never a problem at school, either academically or in terms of behaviour. So, no one asked any awkward questions and I was left with my secrets intact.

I was lucky that I was surrounded by a very supportive group of fellow students at High School. They allowed me to have a normal life at school as long as I made sure there was never more than minimal crossover with home. None of them knew what was going on at home. There was too much shame attached to this secret. Even my best friend since Year 8, Chris Prickett, had no idea until years later when we had both nearly finished Year 12.

I was always reasonably bright at school, although not necessarily the best in the class. When I did my Higher Schools Certificate (HSC) in 1973, only a third of the students that had started with me in Year 7 were still there. And only half of those were expected to pass their final exams. Even less would be offered a place at university. I had a very good memory and study came easily to me. I didn't really have to work that hard until I was at university.

In the year I was doing my HSC, my father had a major stroke and was paralysed down the left side. Despite hospital care and some months of rehabilitation, he never recovered. My mother's mental health was relatively stable at this time largely because she was being treated with regular injections

My father later in life

and she couldn't wean herself off the medication. It was still a bit risky keeping my father's insulin in the fridge at home in case she just decided to throw it out one day. Also, he needed nursing care, and help with eating, showering and dressing, which wasn't really possible at home in those days. So, he went into nursing home care until he died about 18 months later. The stroke changed his personality and affected his memory so that he was no longer the same person I had known growing up. He started to smoke again and thought he was still in Palestine.

Firstly, my father was in a large hospital in the city so I could take the train to visit him. Then he was transferred to a rehabilitation centre in Cheltenham, which was a long way away and had no easy public transport connections to my home. In the early months, my cousin Sigi would drive us to see him but that couldn't go on for ever. For over a year, I visited him once a week by bus and train, which took about an hour and a half each way, until I got my driver's licence. My father passed away in October 1974, my first year at university.

I did well enough in my HSC to be offered my first choice: a place in the Arts Faculty at Monash University. I had hoped to get a Teaching Studentship for university, which would have given me enough money to leave home and live in the university halls of residence. It was not to be. I was offered a scholarship and a place at Rusden Secondary Teachers College, where I couldn't study languages or become a languages teacher.

The Whitlam Government abolished university tuition fees from 1974 and introduced a means tested living allowance for all students. I decided to go to Monash University even though it meant staying at home and a lot less money. “Gough’s Gift” not only allowed me to go to university but also gave me the means to do so.

A university education

I was one of the first few people in my immediate family to go to university. My brother Walter and my cousin Sigi had only gone to night school at Swinburne Technical College after finishing their apprenticeships. Only my mother’s first cousin, Hartmann Trefz, had done a Commerce Degree at the University of Melbourne in the 1950s and he worked in a bank. In Germany, my first cousin Ilse, on my father’s side, also went to university. She studied economics in the 1960s and eventually worked for the German Reserve Bank (*Bundesbank*).

Graduation as Master of Arts in 1986.

At Monash, I studied German, English and Classical Literature, Philosophy and Linguistics, graduating with Honours in German in 1977. I had planned to become a secondary German teacher since my early teens but soon became convinced that language teaching should start much earlier, preferably in kindergarten or early primary school.

I won a scholarship from the German government to study for a semester at the University of Trier in Germany during my fourth (Honours) year. In 1978, I completed a primary teaching diploma. In 1979, I returned to Monash to study for a Master's Degree in German Linguistics, which I was awarded in 1986.

Again, at university, I had a very supportive group of friends and fellow students, some of whom became life-long friends. It was a lot easier to hide the secret of my crazy mother as there was far less contact between home and family, and my life at university. I managed to leave home for a year in 1975 but had to go back because I could no longer afford it. I studied in Germany for part of my Honours year, so I wasn't home all that much anyway.

In my fourth year at university, I won a scholarship from the German government to study for one semester at the University of Trier in Germany. This was my first ever experience overseas. While my German was quite good in those days, my communicative competence was almost nil. I couldn't make simple transactions, such as buy a train ticket, order and pay for a meal, or purchase something in a shop. You need to use certain standard expressions to do these things properly and politely. I remember wandering around the railway station in Zürich for about an hour when I first arrived, trying to work out how to buy a ticket to Nuremberg (*Nürnberg*), where my brother lived. I did finally buy that ticket, but I'm sure I asked for it so clumsily that I was immediately marked as a foreigner.

I had always planned to go back to Germany after I graduated from university and had worked a few years, much as my brother Walter had done. I grew up in two worlds; one set in the reality of where I lived; the other in Germany where my father's family and my brother lived and that I had heard about all my life. There was also this world called Palestine where the Templers had lived but which no longer existed. I never entirely belonged in the Australia I grew up in.

When I finally spent about six months travelling and studying in Germany, I discovered I didn't belong there either. No one treated me like a German, not even my family, even though my German was good and my accent was genuine. My brother said that I just didn't look like a German. And having not grown up there, I didn't have the cultural knowledge and sensitivities either. It was a bit of a shock realising that I couldn't just fit in there like I wanted to. When I returned to Australia I finished my degree and then studied for a Diploma in Primary Education and became a primary teacher. After I started work, I left home for good.

I want to join the Labor Party!

That's what I said when I walked into the Boronia campaign office for Tony Lamb, Labor MHR for LaTrobe in November 1975. That night I went to my first Branch meeting and for the next month I did letterboxing, doorknocking, and handed out leaflets in shopping centres for the election campaign. Outraged at the sacking of the Whitlam government by the then Governor General, Sir John Kerr, I joined the Australian Labor Party (ALP). Joining a political party, especially one on the Left, was frowned upon in my wider family and community, given their experiences in WW2. But for me, it was the right thing to do.

The first time I voted was in 1974, thanks to Prime Minister Whitlam lowering of the voting age to 18. With a few friends, I went to see him at an election rally at the former Ferntree Gully Technical School Hall. It was packed to the rafters. I remember the organisers wouldn't give us posters (coreflutes) to hold up because we weren't party members and they didn't quite trust us. The atmosphere was electric and we shouted and screamed for Gough as loudly as we could. One of my friends even shook his hand.

The Vietnam War and Australia's involvement in it was a major issue for my generation. I was too young to go to most of the early Vietnam War Moratorium marches but I did go to one of the last ones. The young men I went to high school with, did Year 12 with, were the next group due to be conscripted into the army and sent to Vietnam. (It was only 18 year old young men that were conscripted; not women.) There was a ballot and if a marble with the date of your birthday on it was pulled out, you had to report for military training. After their basic training these young conscripts were sent to fight and die in Vietnam.

Although the ALP had originally supported Australia's involvement in Vietnam, they eventually opposed it. Dr Jim Cairns was instrumental in the ant-war movement, as were many in the Labor Party, and he led the Moratorium marches. One of Gough Whitlam's first acts in government after winning the 1972 federal election, was to end conscription and bring home the last of our troops from Vietnam.

The 1975 federal election outcome was a great disappointment. Everyone I knew was voting for Labor but the greater majority of Australians didn't. While many didn't like the way Gough was sacked by the Governor General, they had had enough of a government that didn't seem to know what it was doing and was lurching from one crisis to the next. The 1977 election was an even greater disappointment. The vote against Labor was even greater than it had been in 1975, just in case we hadn't heard them.

At the 1976 State election, a young Steve Crabb won the seat of Knox in the Victorian Legislative Assembly and held it for the next 16 years until he retired undefeated in 1992 as a senior Minister in the Cain-Kirner government. I worked on Steve's campaigns and learnt a lot from him. I also learnt a lot about being in the Labor Party. I was on Branch and Federal Electorate Assembly (FEA) executives, local state electorate and FEA campaign committees, policy committees, an FEA delegate to ALP State Conference and the Public Office Selection Committee which preselects the Party's candidates for election.

In those days, the Boronia Branch, of which I was a member, had about 120 members and over 60 people would attend an ordinary monthly Branch meeting. There was a guest speaker at every meeting and the Branch would pass motions on all sorts of policy issues and send them off to all and sundry to take action on important issues. It would not last; by the early 1990s the Branch could and sometimes did meet in someone's car.

I had become disillusioned with the infighting and factionalism that had crept into the local Labor Party. After all, I had lots of other things to do. At the first meeting that I went to after having been in another Branch for a few years, it was clear to me that which side of the room you sat on now depended on your faction. For some years, I only renewed my membership because a trusted friend convinced me to do so. Eventually, I returned. Someone said to me that there wouldn't be a local Labor Party any more if people like me didn't come back.

An identity in Multiculturalism

When I returned from Germany in 1977, I got involved in the German and other ethnic communities, thanks to my Masters supervisor, good friend and mentor, Professor Michael Clyne, from Monash University. Michael had run the Education Committee of the Association of German Speaking Communities (AGSC) for some time and wanted someone else to take it over. He called a meeting of current and former students and others and before I knew it, I was the new Chair.

The AGSC had been formed in the early-1970s to advocate for the interests of Germans in Australia and to work together with other ethnic communities to further the needs and interests of non-English speaking background Australians. It had an Education Committee and a Media Committee, which had a German program on public radio 3ZZ until the station was closed down by the Fraser federal government. Through the AGSC. I learnt about the Ethnic Communities' Council of Victoria (ECCV) and the Federation of Ethnic Community Councils of Australia (FECCA).

One day, I was called to a meeting to talk about setting up an Education Committee for the ECCV. I didn't really know much about the ECCV but given that German always had to fight for a place among other ethnic communities and to be called a community language, I thought I had better bring some support. I thought bringing three or four people would make sure we could hold our own if we had to.

We duly turned up to this meeting in Carlton at Co.As. It. (the Italian Assistance Association). They even had their own building with a boardroom! In attendance were one representative each of the Australian Greek Welfare Society (AGWS), the Maltese Community Council of Victoria, Co.As. It., and FILEF (the Federation of Italian Migrant Workers and their Families) and then there were four Germans from the AGSC. They sat along one side of the boardroom table and we on the other. We sized each other up across the table! In the end, we agreed to keep working together in an Education Committee under the ECCV. Years later, I learned that they were all quite as intimidated by us as we were by them. We had turned up with four people when they could barely scrape up one each. I learnt a really valuable lesson that day.

In the more than 12 years I was involved with ethnic communities, I held a number of positions, including Education Committee Chair, Secretary, FECCA Delegate and Deputy and Acting President. I wrote policy and funding submissions and joined delegations to Ministers. I made two presentations to the Senate Inquiry into a National Policy on Languages. The ECCV fought for the creation of the Special Broadcasting Service television and for Radio 3ZZZ to replace the former 3ZZ.

I realised that I had more in common with Greek-Australians and Italian-Australian than I did with Anglo-Australians. The migration experience and growing up as the child of immigrants has a lot in common regardless of the cultural background you come from. My language teacher training students would tell me how their friends who only spoke English would expect them to be able to understand and translate any other language regardless of what it was and what language they actually knew. Those who only speak English sometimes have some quite strange ideas. No bilingual would ever think such a ridiculous thing!

Languages and bilingual education

When federal Galbally Report funding was made available through State and Territory level committees, Professor Michael Clyne thought the time was right to try and set up a bilingual program in a primary school. Michael would coordinate the research and evaluation, which would compare a number of subjects taught in German with a typical second language teaching program. Syndal North PS would just teach German language and Bayswater South PS would teach some subjects in German in Years 1 and 3. These were Social Studies, Science,

Music, Art and Physical Education. Each subject contributed different kinds of language skills to the children's' learning.

Barbara Imberger was the German teacher and taught only in German from the first school day of term 1, 1981. Over the years, the program grew throughout the school and some of the subjects changed. Many of Professor Michael Clyne's graduate students, including me, did research projects at the school. It allowed the program to be fine-tuned as needed. Parents were regularly briefed on progress. Class teachers and principals grew to respect it. There were many German teachers who have worked in the bilingual program over the years, many children who have benefited from it. Class teachers and principals came to champion it. Research was published all over the world. It became and still is a showcase and a model for how languages could be taught differently and learnt better.

That's how a small experimental bilingual program began at Bayswater South Primary School. It is still going over 40 years later. It is not necessarily the same as it was at the beginning. It is not the same as either Barbara or I would run it. It's still a very good German program though and it is now totally imbedded in the school. It is a lasting tribute to all of those of us who dared to dream all those years ago that it was possible. But it is a special tribute to Professor Michael Clyne and Barbara Imberger-Sonntag, who really made it happen at the beginning. They both passed away in 2010.

Stopping Kerr's quarry

In 1986, I moved into my own home in Ferntree Gully, in the foothills of the Dandenong Ranges, about two streets from the National Park. It was a lovely bush block with trees and birds and wildlife (mostly possums!). A family of kookaburras still visits every few years. It was a quiet and peaceful place, except for every day the quarry was working.

Kerr's Quarry had been at the end of my street since 1928, but by the 1960s and 1970s it had grown into a large open-cut mine. For decades, local people had complained. During the daily blasting, the houses shook, the windows rattled and babies woke up screaming. Dust seeped into and covered everything inside people's homes. People also worried about their safety when a blast sent a huge rock into a nearby backyard knocking down a large tree branch. Rock was trucked along local roads passing a kindergarten, two schools and a residential aged care home. Rocks and stones spilled onto roads breaking some car windscreens. There was also the constant noise of the rock crusher.

The quarry responded to some concerns; lining the crusher reduced the noise, spraying water when it was dry reduced the dust, but didn't remove these problems. Alarms alerted the locals to upcoming blasting. Tarpaulins were installed on trucks, but rocks continued to fall from trucks and tarpaulins were often missing or just not used.

In the 1970s a local woman took the quarry to court but failed to stop the quarrying and another licence extension was granted. When the quarry owner wanted yet another licence extension in the late 1980s, neighbours, Cathy and Bill McCallum and I, formally set up the Ferntree Gully Residents' Action Group (FTG RAG) to stop them once and for all. Along with about 150 locals, we held meetings, made plans, organised petitions and protest marches, and went to Knox City Council meetings. We recorded the details of explosions and trucks without tarpaulins. Regular letters and media releases were sent to the local papers, outlining our concerns. Everyone brought their various skills but many just wanted to help.

The FTG RAG's campaign was determined and relentless. Derryn Hinch's current affairs program ran a story on the community's protest. Councillor Frank Johnson, a long time Councillor and two-time Mayor was persuaded and had a Knox Council decision to support another licence extension reversed. The FTG RAG presented a detailed submission to the Extractive Industries Board and a petition of over 1000 signatures to the Minister for Industry and Economic Planning. In 1991, the Minister approved only two more years of quarrying. The quarry then appealed the Minister's decision to the Administrative Appeals Tribunal (AAT), claiming to have already addressed resident concerns and that closure would lead to unemployment for workers. The AAT Appeal was heard in 1992.

The FTG RAG first had to convince the AAT that we should be allowed to take part in the Hearing, along with Knox City Council and the Shire of Sherbrooke. The quarry had a Queens Council and a team of solicitors. We had nothing like that. As the Appeal dragged on and legal costs escalated, the quarry suggested a negotiation to see if an acceptable agreement could be reached. I represented the FTG RAG.

The AAT case was ultimately settled by agreement. The quarry could continue to quarry for two more years and then had to rehabilitate the site. The community got a commitment that the site would become housing (not a rubbish tip!) and that the giant hole in the ground would become a lake with a community park. Some amenities for the park and safety features for the lake and the cliff face were also agreed to. The park would then be given to Knox City Council for community use. Council later negotiated further concessions and received grants from local Members of Parliament to improve the park.

It took hard and persistent work over a number of years by people who all had other full-time jobs and mortgages to pay.

We succeeded because we never gave up; we paid attention to the details, analysed documents and kept thorough records. We never let the quarry get away with a false or misleading claim without challenging them. And we effectively used and organised the skills and resources in our community.

Languages in the 1990s

In 1983, Robert Fordham, Education Minister in John Cain's newly elected Labor Government, provided an extra 50 teachers to teach community languages in government primary schools. Over the next few years, this was increased to 130 teachers. Ten years later, the Kennett Government was elected on a program of ruthlessly cutting and selling off education and other government services. Schools were closed. Trains and trams were privatised and so were gas and electricity. Only water remained in public hands.

But Kennett's Education Minister, Don Hayward, was committed to improving the teaching of languages, and he himself spoke Italian. Kennett himself supported multiculturalism. Despite all the slashing and burning, $2 million suddenly appeared in 1994 for the teaching languages. The Commonwealth was also investing in languages, especially Asian languages. The National Policy on Languages was getting off the ground. So was a National Asian Languages and Studies in Australian Schools (NALSAS) program, conceived by a young Queensland bureaucrat named Kevin Rudd.

It was a high point for languages other than English (LOTE). Under the management and leadership of Dina Guest, there were about 50 staff, including some provided through agreements with overseas governments. I managed LOTE but we also had an English as a Second Language (ESL) and a Multicultural team. We had languages consultants and advisors to support teachers and provide them with professional development. We commissioned universities to provide retraining courses for existing teachers to increase the supply. We made language teaching materials and broadcast language teaching programs through satellite television. We worked together with the universities and the Catholic and Independent Schools sectors, as well as the consular corps. We also oversaw policy for the after-hours language programs of the Victorian School of Languages (VSL) and the community language schools. We also collected and reported detailed information on all language teaching programs in government schools. There were major LOTE and ESL conferences. Even an advertisement promoting language learning was made and screened on commercial television.

Sadly, it would not last; not for long enough to imbed languages teaching into schools. Dina gained a promotion to another area and I was preselected as a candidate in the 2002 State election. There were people and forces that had long wanted the focus on languages to be gone. Languages was seen to have too much power and command too many resources in the central administration of the Education Department. Also, Commonwealth funding was coming to an end and State government resources were wanted for other priorities. By the time I was elected to parliament, a major restructure was on the horizon. All that we had built over 10 years gradually disappeared. Many of the people soon followed.

15. Playing real politics

I had always planned to run for political office, once I felt I had learned enough and the time was right. In 2002, 27 years after joining the ALP, I did just that. I believed I now had enough experience to give it a go.

Steve Crabb's former seat of Knox had been redistributed for the 2002 election and was now called Ferntree Gully. Liberal Member of Parliament, Hurtle Lupton, had held Knox since 1992 and it was known in the community that he didn't particularly want to run for another term. He was persuaded to run again as he was the best chance the Liberals had of holding the seat. He could then perhaps retire sometime during the next term. My plan was to bring down his 7.6 percent margin at the 2002 election and then win the by-election when he retired. The time was right!

Don't worry, I won't win!

I was duly preselected as the Labor candidate for Ferntree Gully in September of 2002. It was the second batch of candidates preselected for the 30 November election. The first group of a dozen or so marginal seat candidates (the ones with a real chance of winning) had already been campaigning for some time. I had nominated for Monbulk in the first group, but then withdraw my nomination. I then stood for Ferntree Gully when the other 10 or so seats that still needed candidates were preselected. Monbulk was a more winnable seat but Ferntree Gully was where I had lived all my life and I knew it so well. When I announced in the local papers that I was the Labor candidate for Ferntree Gully, many of the local Templers were stunned.

Only a handful of people know about Labor's internal polling. The prevailing wisdom is that telling candidates about their polling results is counter-productive: If they are winning, they will become complacent and stop working, and if they are losing, they will give up and stop working. So, candidates aren't told anything!

Internal polling must have shown Labor's chances had improved. Suddenly, two more seats were about to be lifted into the 'winnable' group: one was Ferntree Gully. This meant that campaign support and resources would flow from the Party. For a month I worked for the Education Department during the day and campaigned at night till about 2.00am. I spoke to my immediate boss, Dina Guest, who was overseas at the time and told her I was going to take leave to campaign full-time until the election as soon as she came back. If the Party was going to invest in me, then I had to do the same. I told her, "Don't worry, I won't win!"

I put out a glossy, full colour introductory leaflet with my own money. I knocked on doors, had street stalls in shopping centres and handed out balloons to children, stood at train stations in the early mornings and put out media releases to the local papers. With our volunteers, we letterboxed and handed out leaflets, bookmarks and cards. In the last week, material just turned up in people's letterboxes, sent out by the central campaign. This was a clear sign that the polling was showing we were doing more than OK.

The biggest job on Election Day is to have enough people to hand out 'how-to-vote' cards and to scrutineer during the count. Together with the regulars, I called on everyone I knew and somehow we covered all the 120 or so by 2 hour shifts. And better still, almost everyone turned up.

Election night with fireworks

The 2002 election was a landslide for Labor. It was a classic second term election. Premier Steve Bracks ran a thoughtful government and people liked what they saw. They were prepared to vote him in for another term because he put money into the things they cared about, including education and health. In 1999, we had won a lot of country seats on the back of the Kennett government having largely ignored country Victoria. In 2002, we won the outer eastern and south eastern suburbs, including Ferntree Gully.

A friend of mine was scrutineering for the first time ever and was on her own at the Heany Park PS polling booth. She rang me on election night, saying: You've won! You've won! After confirming that she was still in the polling booth, I said to her: Don't you dare leave until you have final figures from the Returning Officer! (Once you leave, you cannot go back in.)

By 8.00pm, I had won. It was almost a 10 percent swing. I had a narrow margin, only 2.3 percent, but it was enough to build on and a win is a win is a win!

The 'after party' for my campaign workers was in my basement at home. People were coming and going all night. It had started to drizzle. Somebody asked if they could let off some fireworks. Two volunteers from the local fire brigade were there and gave the go-ahead.

I was on the phone for the next three hours: people I hadn't heard from for years, rang to congratulate me. I think Hurtle Lupton, the sitting member, rang to concede but I dropped the phone as it was handed to me. I was standing on the coffee table making a speech to my volunteers at the time. When I picked up the phone, the line was dead. Hurtle never spoke to me for the next two and a half years.

At midnight we ordered more pizza!

Factions, Caucus and Getting Started

On the Monday after the election, factions meetings began to be held to carve up the spoils of the Labor victory. The Government and the Parliament needed to get to work as soon as possible. The Ministry had to be confirmed, the Whips put into place for both Houses, and Parliamentary Committees set up.

As a new Member of Parliament (MP) I was still mostly feeling shock and awe. At my first Left Faction meeting I was sitting around the table with the likes of Peter Batchelor, Lynne Kosky and John Pandazopoulos, who were all senior ministers. The Factions would discuss and nominate their candidates for various positions and the Premier would later allocate portfolios. (In reality, of course, the Premier had a fair bit of say on who was put forward in the first place.) I had already been lobbied by four people on my way to the meeting.

At my first Labor Caucus meeting a few days later, the Government was keen to show it was getting on with the job. The Premier introduced all the newly elected MPs. Actually, some MPs had not even been confirmed elected yet. Counting was still underway in Heather McTaggert's seat of Evelyn. When it came to my turn, he slightly mispronounced my name; understandable really. It had been happening all my life, so I instinctively corrected the Premier's pronunciation.

After the meeting, we were all ushered to the front steps of Parliament for a media photograph of the Caucus. On the way there, John Pandazopoulos came over to me grinning and commented on how I had corrected the Premier. "Start as you mean to go on", I said, trying to sound confident.

On the steps, Carolyn Hirsh grabbed me and said, "Come on, we need to get in the middle, towards the front so we can be seen". She was right. Nobody sees who is in the back row.

Reform of the Legislative Council

Not only was Labor re-elected with an increased majority in Legislative Assembly, we had won a majority in the Legislative Council. The first order of business for the re-elected Labor Government was to reform the Upper House: There would be no more frustrating the Government's legislation!

Sitting in Parliament.

I couldn't speak in parliament until I had given my inaugural speech, which wasn't until the 20th March 2003. There were so many new members that it took quite a number of sitting weeks to get through everyone. If you get caught interjecting before that, you are fair game for the Opposition to interject on your actual inaugural speech, which otherwise is not allowed.

As I couldn't yet speak in the House, I spent a lot of my early sitting weeks in the chamber, watching and learning how things were done. I also listened to a lot of the debates in the Legislative Council, especially on the legislation to reform the Upper House. We had the numbers to pass the legislation through both houses but the Opposition fought it every step of the way.

Before the election, Labor had promised the Greens Party that if it won a majority in both Houses, the Government would reform the Legislative Council by introducing proportional representation voting for Upper House elections. This would significantly improve the chances for Greens Party candidates to be elected. As a result, the Greens preferenced Labor on their How-to-Vote cards in 2002. Never a good deed goes unpunished and this one came back to bite us.

Inaugural speech to parliament[113]

Even though I had had a lot of experience in public speaking, the prospect of speaking in parliament and all the rules that needed to be followed, worried me at the beginning. I suffered from a certain amount of 'Imposter Syndrome', having never really believed I would win the election.

You don't get into parliament by yourself and I certainly had help from many friends, family and the local comrades.

113 See Appendix 1

I was due to give my inaugural speech on the evening of the 19th of March 2003. I organised a dinner in parliament's Strangers Corridor for about a dozen or so people; family and close friends who had supported me. Afterwards they waited patiently in the gallery to hear me give my inaugural speech and I waited patiently to give it. As the night wore on and other things intervened, it looked as if my inaugural speech wasn't going to happen that night. I had to tell them all to go home and finally gave it the next day. A few former work colleagues from the Education Department came across to watch me deliver it.

Speaking in the Victorian Legislative Assembly

My office in parliament house was on the third floor. There was a beautiful view over the city from the roof. You had to go up a rickety lift, up another flight of stairs, along a rickety steep walkway which went over the dome to the parliamentary library and along another concrete path. Alternatively, you could go down to the second floor by way of a narrow set of concrete spiral stairs. The Victorian Parliament House was not built for women MPs with heels.

Although the steep walkway over the library dome had a handrail, it was the worst part of the journey, especially when running to the House for a Division. One day, I slipped on the steep walkway and nearly broke my ankle. I got no sympathy from the Speaker, who proceeded to point out the total unsuitability of my shoes. There was nothing for it but to wear sensible shoes in parliament.

The time available for speaking in parliament has to be carefully managed otherwise nothing would get done. Each sitting week, I would put forward a list of the things I wanted to speak on. Nothing was certain of course, because there were 61 other government MPs also putting forward their own lists. Sometimes almost everyone wanted to speak on a Bill and a lot would miss out. It was more likely that you would get to speak on some obscure piece of legislation than on things you really cared about. You might also be asked to cut your contribution down to a few minutes rather than get the allotted 10 minutes.

Members' statements at the beginning of the day gave you 90 seconds to talk about anything, but mainly about people or things happening in your electorate. Grievance statements let you complain about something and Matters of Public Importance restricted you to a specific topic. The Adjournment Debate allowed members to raise issues of concern with Ministers and if you were lucky, the Minister would be in the Chamber and give you an answer straight away. You could then send a copy of the Hansard to people interested or affected by the issue. If the Minister was not in the Chamber, you would get the answer in writing some time later.

When not in the Chamber, MPs are kept busy with going to meetings and briefings, preparing for their speeches in the House and writing media releases to the local papers, keeping in touch with what is going on in the electorate and the electorate office, and making phone calls. When a Division is called, you have three minutes to get into the Chamber before the doors are locked and you have to vote. Never miss a Division!

Ferntree Gully, the best electorate ever

I inherited the former member's electorate office in Mountain Gate. It was a busy little shopping centre in the middle of the electorate. The air conditioning and the heating didn't work properly, and the furniture dated from the 1970s. But, it was a good location that would be useful in getting wider recognition in the community.

My electorate office at the Mountain Gate Shopping Centre

I accepted every invitation to visit a community group I could, the only exceptions being for parliamentary sitting days, parliamentary committee activities, or clashes with other commitments in the electorate. On weekends, I would always have lots of appointments.

Working in the electorate office

Setting up the electoral office was relatively easy. Robyn Burke, my Personal Assistant, had worked for both Steve Crabb and Jenny Macklin (federal Member for Jagajaga) for many years and was very experienced. Christmas was almost upon us when we finally got into the office so there was some quiet time in early January to set up the office and the systems. Unfortunately, we had no working computers until the end of January when Parliamentary Services finally got around to setting them all up.

Most people are courteous and appreciate what you are doing to try to help them. Unfortunately, there are always a very small number that think they can say anything they want to you, 'because they pay your salary and you have to do what they want".

Very early on as an MP, a constituent came to see me with his partner. I don't even remember what it was about. "Now how do we address you?" he said. I clearly looked puzzled. "What do we call you?" he tried again. "You call me Anne", I said, "because that's my name." I will always remember this generous and humble person.

The issues that people bring to their local MP are many and varied. They also don't distinguish between the responsibilities of different levels of government. You have to learn quickly where to get the information you need to help your constituents.

Not all issues were even about State government services, although roads, schools, health and disability services were quite common. On the other hand, concerns about the local Knox City Council such as planning, local roads and footpaths, kindergartens and even local bus routes, were very common. Immigration issues, were of course a Federal responsibility. People also want advice on a lot of personal problems, including: financial counselling, taxation, and employment disputes. It is a real privilege to be trusted with people's problems and to try to help them sort them out.

Early on, Robyn asked me about my football team. She said that I would get all sorts of things from the team. The look on my face must have said it all. This is not what I got into politics for. I'll tell them you haven't got one, she said tactfully. The next thing I know, I am in the daily papers as the 'one brave Victorian MP' who will actually admit to not supporting a footy team! A few weeks later a package arrived from the Western Bulldogs, saying they noticed I didn't have a football team and they wondered if I would consider supporting them. They had included two free memberships. We gave the memberships to a couple of local Bulldogs fans. In Melbourne, it seems you really can't get away with not having a footy team.

The Endeavour Awards

I started the Endeavour Award for schools in my electorate. From 2003, a boy and a girl in years 6 and 10 were selected by each school for the award. The award was not necessarily for the academically best student, but for the one who had tried very hard all year and/or had made an important contribution to the school community. I gave each school a perpetual shield which they could engraved with the names of the winners. Students each received a hardcover book with a bookplate in the front signed by me. I then presented the award at a school assembly or graduation event.

Presenting the 2003 Endeavour Award at Ferntree Gully North PS

The books were all by Australian authors or about the lives and achievements of well-known young Australians. They were carefully chosen to appeal to the student's age group and interests.

One year, a member of my staff opened the secondary school book for that year at several pages at random and read aloud a few passages containing some rather colourful but inappropriate language. I was really quite shocked, but there was nothing to be done as we had already given out the books. We all held our breaths! I didn't get a single complaint, but perhaps the students, and moreover their parents, never actually read the books.

The Endeavour Awards even survived me as the local MP. Some schools continued to present them long after I lost the 2006 election. I know of one school who even got my Liberal Party successor to present them for years afterwards. Long after I left parliament, kids would let me know that they had received one of my awards when they saw me somewhere, such as on the street or at the supermarket.

Gough Whitlam is on the phone for you

One day, I came back into the office and everyone looked a bit pale and shocked. It's Gough Whitlam on the phone for you, said one of my electorate staff. I have to say I was a little surprised myself. Some weeks earlier, I had written to Gough to thank him for enabling me to go to university all those years ago and to tell him how I had turned out.[114]

Gough thanked me for my letter which was on my letterhead as MP for Ferntree Gully. He said he rang me up because my phone number was at the top. We talked for a long time about the rally at Ferntree Gully Tech in 1974 where I had first seen him, about me going to university because his government had abolished university fees and about me now being a Labor MP in the Victorian Parliament. I thanked him again.

It was a very special experience and I will always remember it!

---

114 See Appendix 2

Parliamentary Education and Training Committee

Committee work is actually an opportunity to work with other MPs across Party lines. Parliamentary Committees hold inquiries, hear from witnesses, consult with experts in the field and report to the parliament on their findings. Sometimes the Government will make a referral to a Parliamentary Committee on an issue it wants some advice on; at other times, the committee will itself come up with the issue to be looked into.

Parliamentary Education and Training Committee MPs Steve Herbert, me, Nick Kotsiras, Helen Buckingham, Victor Perton and Janice Munt

The Parliamentary Education and Training Committee, of which I was a member, was a new committee set up by the 55th Parliament and was chaired by Steve Herbert, Member for Eltham and former chief of staff to the Education Minister, the Hon. Lynne Kosky.

The committee held a number of inquiries and produced four reports to Parliament:

- Inquiry into the Impact of Unmet Demand for Higher Education, presented 2nd June 2004

- Inquiry into the Suitability of Pre-service Teacher Training Courses presented 28th February 2005
- Inquiry into the Promotion of Maths and Science Education, presented 2nd March 2006
- Inquiry into the Effects of Television and Multimedia on Education in Victoria, presented 4th October 2006.

I was especially proud of our report into Pre-service Teacher Training Courses, which called out the universities on the poor quality of some of their courses and especially the inadequate support for trainee teachers in practical classroom teaching. The universities were not happy, but I called it out as I saw it and as the schools in my electorate told me they saw it too.

You've worked hard, you deserve to get back

2006 was re-election year. It was full on campaigning all year. As well, the Commonwealth Games were held in Melbourne in March of that year.

The tolling of the Scoresby Freeway, announced back in 2003, continued to grate with voters in my electorate, especially in Rowville. And the Liberals never let them forget it!

The Government had promised at the 2002 election that there would be no tolls on the Scoresby Freeway (now called EastLink). Unfortunately, the operator of half of Melbourne's train system, privatised by the former Kennett government, walked away and handed back the keys shortly after the election. The Government could not let half of Melbourne's trains just stop running. It would take billions of dollars for the government to take back the running of these trains. For one thing, there were no staff left in the Department who knew how to do it.

There was no money left for a toll free Scoresby Freeway

after bailing out the trains. And despite all my positive efforts, Ferntree Gully voters never quite forgot or forgave us.

Ferntree Gully was a great electorate. That is not to say that representing it wasn't sometimes difficult and challenging. The community was largely supportive, especially in the northern areas of Boronia and Ferntree Gully. Conservative Rowville was always a challenge but I worked very hard to get them funding for road projects and traffic lights as well as the new Smart Bus route to Oakleigh. I also got approval and funding for three major school upgrades: Kent Park, Mountain Gate and Karoo primary schools.

On election day, I was handing out How-to-Vote cards in the late afternoon at one of the bigger and more conservative polling booths at Karoo PS, when one of the prominent local Liberals said to me: You've worked hard, Anne, you deserve to get back. It was not to be!

27 f***ing votes

The 2006 election was held on the 25th of November. There was no definitive result in Ferntree Gully on the night. It took almost 3 weeks of counting and recounting, three full recounts and the Chief Retuning Officer supervising the final recount and ruling votes in or out in terms of formality, to get the final result. I lost by 27 f***ing votes.

I had another week to clear out the electorate office and return the car, the laptop and the mobile phone. It was almost Christmas and I had no job, no income, no car, not even a mobile phone. I had a mortgage to pay and cats to feed. For a while we were eating the house!

After I lost the 2006 election, it took me the next 18 months to feel normal again.

* * *

For the 2022 election, the Division of Ferntree Gully was abolished and split between the electorates of Rowville, Monbulk and Bayswater. A nice young politician named Jackson Taylor held the redistributed seat of Bayswater over a challenge from my Liberal opponent from 2006. I really celebrated long and hard that night.

* * *

It was both an honour and a privilege to serve!

16. Storylines to the present

I grew up as the child of immigrants from a far off land, a very long way away from most of my German ancestors. Migrant kids tend to grow up tough or they go under. I have been lucky to have inherited some of the genes of the strong women and men that came before me.

My great grandmother, Katharina Graf, travelled to a foreign land in the orient in 1873 as a 16 year old teenager with her stepsister, not knowing what to expect when they got there. Just over 30 years later, my grandmother Anna Barbara Trefz did the same, but alone and at the age of 15. My other great grandmother Catharina Aichele raised two children as a single mother in a small village in the Black Forest in the 1890s. They all did remarkable things, particularly for their times.

While I knew something of my mother's parents and grandparents, I didn't know much about my Eckstein family in Germany until I began to explore their stories later in life. They were mostly stonemasons and farmers. They were also active in their church communities and in local government. I have only gotten to know something of the Kunstmann story quite recently. The Kunstmanns, or the males at least, were well educated going back to the 17th and 18th centuries. They were theologians and ministers of religion, doctors and engineers.

I have always believed in 'nurture' over 'nature'; and that we all make our own way in life rather than being predestined by our ancestry. But, I cannot ignore what the lives of my ancestors have to tell me. I can see myself in their lives down the generations and how they manifest in my own life.

I can now see that my interest in politics comes from the Eckstein mayors of Rosstal. The interest in history, languages, philosophy and religions comes from the Kunstmann theologians and protestant ministers, even though I didn't inherit their Christian beliefs. The academic skills come from the Kunstmanns; the practical and technical skills come from all the farmers and tradespeople down the generations. The love of travel and sense of adventure comes from my father and my Templer ancestors.

Also, my amazing father's achievements should not be forgotten. He taught me about the importance of truth, values and loyalty; and about persistence in the face of hardship. He loved literature and the world of the imagination. As a child, he told me beautiful stories of elves and dwarfs in the forest, the Arabian nights, and ancient Norse myths and legends. I'm sure his genes also played a big part in how I turned out.

Appendix 1: Inaugural Speech to Parliament

Victorian Legislative Assembly
Governor's Speech: Address-In-Reply
20 March 2003

Ms ECKSTEIN (Ferntree Gully)[115] – It is my great honour and pleasure to address this house today as the first member for Ferntree Gully. I am indeed proud that the first member for Ferntree Gully is a Labor member, as indeed was the first member for Knox, the former seat on which Ferntree Gully is based.

Acting Speaker, I ask you to pass on my congratulations to the Speaker on her election to this high office. I would also like to congratulate the Premier on his re-election and that of the government in what was an extraordinary show of support and confidence in the government by the Victorian people.

It is indeed an historic occasion that, for the first time, this house has a woman as its Speaker, as well as so many other women members of Parliament. In fact 40 percent of this Bracks government is comprised of women.

To the new women members for Bellarine, Evelyn, Forest Hill, Gembrook, Hastings, Kilsyth, Mill Park, Mordialloc, Mount Waverley and Yan Yean,

115 Hansard, 20/3/2003. Page 470-473

I particularly congratulate you on your election to this house.

It is indeed a great privilege to serve alongside so many extremely capable and talented women parliamentarians. It augurs well for this 55th Parliament being a truly representative place.

I would now like to thank the many people who supported my election to Parliament. Firstly, I thank the voters of Ferntree Gully, who have entrusted me to represent them. It is a great privilege to serve the people of Ferntree Gully, and I shall always endeavour to represent the needs and aspirations of all the people of my electorate. I am deeply honoured to be given the opportunity to serve the people of Ferntree in the Bracks government.

I would also like to thank my campaign team, all the local Labor Party members and supporters, and the many personal friends and work colleagues who worked tirelessly on my election campaign.

In particular, I would like to thank my campaign director, Don Barker, for keeping both me and the campaign on track, and also my very good friend and colleague Carolyn Hirsh, who is now a member for Silvan Province, for her ongoing advice, encouragement and support. I also thank Daniel Andrews, the member for Mulgrave; Lee Tarlamis; and Alan Griffin, the federal member for Bruce, for their support and encouragement.

I also need to acknowledge the extraordinary support of Emily's List for the advice, training and resources provided, which were absolutely invaluable. The encouragement and support given to me by

Joan Kirner, the first and only woman to become Premier of this state, deserves particular mention.

I would now like to pay tribute to an extraordinary woman: my aunt, Ida Katerina Messner, who is now 88 years young. She essentially raised me during the many years of my mother's debilitating mental illness.

I would also like to pay tribute to the role of my father, Johann Konrad Eckstein, who, although he passed away many years ago, shaped many of my values and political views.

He always encouraged me to think for myself about important issues and to question the actions of the conservative state and federal governments of the day, regardless of whether they conflicted with his own views or whether he thought them, or me, particularly wise or prudent at the time.

I remember many lively discussions during my teens on issues such as conservation of the environment and Australia's involvement in the Vietnam War. Fortunately we did agree on most issues, including the need for better health, education and welfare services.

Having come to Australia in 1953 with my mother and older brother, after having survived the war years in Germany and the devastation, both physical and psychological, of post-war Germany, my father valued the freedoms and opportunities that Australia offered to people from all over the world. He had strong political views even though he was understandably diffident about any overt participation in the political process after the tyranny of Nazi Germany.

There his small act of defiance – that of not attending military training at his workplace because he was supposedly attending training at precisely the same time in his local township and failing to go to training in his local township because he was required at training at his workplace, and actually going to neither – could have had dire consequences for both himself and the family, had he ever been found out.

He also valued education very highly and encouraged me to always strive for high academic standards and to continue my education, even when our family's economic circumstances made that quite difficult.

In that regard, I must also acknowledge the extraordinary role of the Whitlam Labor government in abolishing fees for tertiary education. Without 'Gough's gift', I and many other young people from ordinary working-class families would never have had the opportunity to undertake a university education.

My outrage at the Liberal-controlled Senate refusing to pass supply and the subsequent sacking of the Whitlam government in 1975 prompted me to join the Boronia branch of the Australian Labor Party, of which I am still a member.

I am therefore delighted to serve in this Bracks Labor government, whose reforms to the Legislative Council will ensure that supply can never be denied to a Victorian government with a mandate from the people.

As a former primary teacher and manager in the

Department of Education and Training I have a strong interest in and personal commitment to ensuring the best possible educational opportunities and outcomes from our public schools and educational institutions.

Therefore, I am delighted that education – along with health, community safety and the environment – is one of the highest priorities of this Bracks government. I look forward to contributing to improvements in schools and in public education more generally, both for the people of Ferntree Gully and for Victoria as a whole.

My father also encouraged me to value my German heritage and to maintain my first language and culture.

This was not an easy thing to do in the 1950s and 1960s when assimilation was the policy of the day and if you spoke another language in public, people told you to stop.

Schools and teachers actively discouraged parents from speaking languages other than English to their children in the false belief that it would hinder their acquisition of English.

Fortunately, my father ignored these short-sighted and xenophobic views, and as a result I have maintained both the German language and culture.

In that regard I also need to pay tribute to the role of Professor Michael Clyne, now at the University of Melbourne, who not only greatly improved my German language skills but saw me through a Bachelor of Arts (Honours) degree and a Masters degree in German at Monash University.

These days we are all a bit more enlightened and we value the rich cultural and linguistic diversity of our multicultural community. However, there is still more work to be done in ensuring that in the future all young Victorians achieve both high levels of literacy in English and proficiency in at least one other language.

Respect for diversity of values, beliefs and cultural and religious practices within the overall framework of our culturally and linguistically diverse community is one of the guiding principles that I will endeavour to bring to my work as a member of Parliament.

However, as a community we still have much to repair in terms of reconciliation with indigenous Australians. I would therefore like to say 'sorry' to indigenous Australians for the past wrongs that have been committed. I would also like to acknowledge the Kulin nation, the traditional owners of the land on which this Parliament sits as well as the electorate of Ferntree Gully, and to pay my respects to their elders.

Ferntree Gully is a new electorate which includes long-established areas in Boronia, Ferntree Gully and Mountain Gate as well as the more recently developed suburbs of Lysterfield and Rowville. Having lived in the electorate all my life I have seen the area change from small, almost rural townships to cosmopolitan suburbs. While this has brought with it many improved facilities and services, the challenge remains to preserve the leafy character and environment of this area at the foot of the Dandenong Ranges.

While Ferntree Gully is a new electorate, I would like to acknowledge the contribution made to the area by the former member for Knox, Hurtle Lupton, who served as the local member for 10 years. I wish him and his family well in the future and thank him on behalf of the constituents of Ferntree Gully for the work he did during his term in office.

I would also like to acknowledge Steve Crabb who was the first member for Knox. He held the seat for a period of 16 years from 1976 to 1992. Steve made a significant contribution to the community during his time as the local member.

He also provided me personally with lots of support and encouragement to become more active in politics. At the time I was a new and enthusiastic young member of the Labor Party who did not know much about politics but who was passionate about reform and social change. Steve showed me that it was possible to make a difference to ordinary people through participation in the political process.

The issues which concern the people of Ferntree Gully are those which concern all Victorians – that is, health, education, community safety and the environment.

The upgrading of facilities at the Angliss Hospital in Upper Ferntree Gully, provided by the Bracks government, is therefore most welcome.

Also, the 28 extra teachers who are now in schools in the Ferntree Gully electorate as a result of first-term Bracks government initiatives and the improved facilities of schools such as Heany Park, Wattleview and Ferntree Gully North primary schools are also very much appreciated by the community.

The building of a new police station in Rowville is about to commence and will provide enhanced community safety for the people of Rowville and Lysterfield.

I look forward to working as a member of the Bracks government on policies and initiatives in these important community services. However, there is still more work to be done to undo the damage of the former Kennett government to our essential community services.

Protecting our environment is also an important local priority, given the location of the electorate in the foothills of the Dandenongs. The Dandenong Ranges on the eastern boundary of my electorate and the Lysterfield Lake Park in its south-eastern corner are important 'green wedges' which will be protected for future generations as a result of Bracks government policies.

As with other outer suburban areas, there are ongoing challenges in improving roads and public transport in Ferntree Gully as the population and housing development increases. While the older established areas of my electorate in Boronia and Ferntree Gully have access to train and bus services, the newer areas of Rowville and Lysterfield are heavily reliant on cars.

This is putting considerable pressure on the existing road network, much of which needs upgrading to cope effectively with the increased population now living in these areas. Public transport in the newer areas is quite limited, with bus services generally not operating after hours or at weekends.

It is therefore pleasing that the Bracks government has implemented new bus routes in Rowville and committed $100 million to an outer metropolitan roads program.

This and the many other initiatives that the Bracks government will deliver during its second term will undoubtedly benefit not only the people of the electorate of Ferntree Gully but Victorians as a whole.

I am proud to represent the people of Ferntree Gully. I look forward to working constructively with many of you over the life of this Parliament on the many important social issues that will come before us.

Appendix 2: Letter to former Prime Minister Gough Whitlam

ANNE ECKSTEIN MP

State Member for Ferntree Gully

The Hon. Gough Whitlam AC QC
Level 19
Westfield towers
100 William Street
SYDNEY NSW 2011

Dear Gough

For some time, I have wanted to write to you to thank you for what you and your government did for young people like myself in the 1970s and to let you know how that opportunity has benefited me over the years and enabled me to become what I am today.

Without your enlightened policy on free tertiary education, I would never have had the opportunity to study at university. My parents migrated to Australia in the early 1950's and while they always encouraged me to strive for educational excellence, would never have been able to pay for university tuition fees. Because tertiary education was free and an allowance was available through the Tertiary education Assistance Scheme, I was able to complete an Arts Degree with Honours at Monash University in 1977 followed by primary teacher training in 1978. In 1985, after becoming a teacher and working full-time in the Victorian Education Department, I also completed a Masters degree in Arts at Monash. Since graduating from university I have had a very successful 24 year career in education, firstly as a teacher, then as a teacher adviser and finally as a fairly senior manager in the Victorian Department of Education & Training. None of this would have been possible for me had I not gone to university, which I could not have done had I had to pay fees.

Since November 1975, I have also been an active member of the Australian Labor Party. I voted Labor for the first time at the 1974 double dissolution election and remember well your rousing speech at the Ferntree Gully Technical School Hall in 1974 with local member, Tony Lamb. It was the dismissal of your government in November 1975 that prompted me to join the ALP and I have been a member ever since.

Since joining the Party, I have worked for many Labor candidates who stood for La Trobe, Aston or Knox at the federal and state levels. Some like Steve Crabb, State Member for Knox from 1976 to 1982 were successful. Many were not. That is the nature of politics in the outer eastern suburbs of Melbourne.

In 2002, I was preselected for the seat of Ferntree Gully at the forthcoming State election, which required a 7.6 per cent swing to unseat the sitting Liberal member. Although I had no expectations of winning the seat, I was very proud to be a Labor candidate and determined to make the local Liberals work for it. The rest, as they say, is history.

Shop 40, Mountain Gate Shopping Centre, Ferntree Gully 3156
Phone: 9758 6011 Fax: 9758 8053 Email: anne.eckstein@parliament.vic.gov.au

I am now very proud to serve with the 61 other ALP members in the Victorian Legislative Assembly and 25 in the Legislative Council in the Bracks Government. (I enclose a copy of my inaugural speech to the Victorian Parliament for your interest and information.) I am also proud that our government has reformed the Legislative Council so that it will never be able to refuse supply and deny a government with a majority in the people's house the right to govern.

I am very proud to be a member of the Labor Party and to serve the Party and the community as a Labor MP. I firmly believe I would not be in this position had it not been for the progressive policies, as well as the leadership and inspiration you and your government provided to me and my generation. Thank you very much again.

Yours sincerely

Anne Eckstein

ANNE ECKSTEIN MP
State Member for Ferntree Gully

6 April 2004

* Gough Whitlam calls me at the office on 14 April 2004 at 3.45 pm.

Bibliography

Building permit application: Hakius, Georg und Trefz, Jakob vom Kirschenhardthof (Hochberg): Scheunen- und Schuppenanbau, genehmigt am 4.3.1864, Staatsarchiv Ludwigsburg F 210 II Bü 1274

Bürger, Friedrich (Hrg.): *Die evangelische Jakobskirche Mitwitz in Bildern*, Mai 2017

Bürger, Friedrich: *Bilder der Heimat*, Dezember 2007

Damals im Kaukasus: Ein Erzählbuch, published by Tempelgesellschaft Deutschland, Stuttgart, 2001

Evangelische Kirche, Sankt Mauritius, Kirchheim am Neckar *Kirchenbuch 1*

Evangelische Kirche, Sankt Mauritius, Kirchheim am Neckar *Kirchenbuch 2*

Gebäude-Güterbuch der Gemeinde Kirchheim am Neckar

Glenk, Helmut in conjunction with Blaich, Horst and Häring, Manfred: *Desert Sands to Golden Oranges: The History of the German Templer Settlement of Sarona in Palestine from 1871 to 1947*, 2005

Huber, Florian, *Promise me you'll shoot yourself: The mass suicide of ordinary Germans in 1945*, The Text Publishing Company, Melbourne, Australia, 2019

Kirchner, Dr Cornelia: -Feyerabend: *Rosstaler Lebensbilder, Bürgermeister Hans Eckstein *8.4.1885, †28.2.1945*, in *Rosstaler Heimatsblaetter No. 57*, 2021

Last Will and Testament of Katharina Trefz née Graf 1908-1916, from German Consulate in Jerusalem now located in the Israeli National Archives in Jerusalem

McInnes, William, 2011, from the Foreword In: *Little Picture / Little Story*, catalogue for Sarah Watt's last photographic exhibition, quoted In: *When I'm gone…*, The Age newspaper, 22 October 2011

Messerle inheritance documents from the German Consulate in Jerusalem now located in the Israeli National Archives in Jerusalem

Origins of the Temple Society, translation of *Wie es zum Tempel kam* by Peter G Hornung, TSA, Melbourne 2003

Paul Sauer, 1991, *The Holy Land Called: The Story of the Temple Society*, translated by Gunhild Henley, published by The Temple Society Melbourne, 1991

Pfarramt Mitwitz: *1567 – 2017: 450 Jahre evangelisch in Mitwitz, Eine Festschrift*

Perkins, Rachel, 2019, (daughter of Charles Perkins), *Boyer Lecture 1*, 2019

Rosstaler Heimatblätter, including:

- Heft 57, 2021:

Stein, Rick: *'Venice to Istanbul'* program and cookbook

Suicides from 1895-1901 and file on the 1893 lawsuit of *Panisel versus Trefz* from the German Consulate in Jerusalem now located in the Israeli National Archives in Jerusalem

The Temple Society: An Overview, TSA, Melbourne, 1986

Trefz, Johann Jakob: *Inventarium*, Stadtarchiv, Kirchheim am Neckar

Treffz, Hannss Ulrich: *Inventarium*, Stadtarchiv, Kirchheim am Neckar

Treffz, Hermann: *Die Ähre, Mitteilungsblatt der Familie Trefz*, Gerlingen bei Stuttgart, hrg. Familienarchiv Trefz, date unknown

Die Warte des Tempels, (auch Süddeutsche Warte, Jerusalemer Warte), published by the Temple Society in Germany since 1845

Wawrzyn, Heidemarie: *Nazis in the Holy Land 1933-1948*, De Gruyter, 2013

Zörner, Brunnhilde, 1993, *Fürstenhof: 600 Jahre Fürstenhof 1393–1993, Geschichte und Geschichten*, published in 1993

Websites:

Ancestry.com.au, including: Eckstein Trefz Family Tree

Markt Roβtal: *Zeittafel zur Geschichte Roβtals seit der ersten schriftlichen Erwähnung, 1792, 1808, and 1806-1813*

Markt Roβtal: *Roβtaler Heimatsblätter 11* (1985), von Richard Preisel, Hans Eckstein

Markt Roβtal: Heimatsbuch von 1928, von Adolf Rohn, Nachbarorte, *Das Schloβ, Das Schulwesen*

Stolpersteine and Günther Demnig's webbsites, including https:*//www.stolpersteine.eu*

Tempelgesellschaft Deutschland: https://www.tempelgesellschaft.de/de/startseite.php and https://www.tempelgesellschaft.de/de/geschichte.php

Temple Society Australia: https://templesociety.org.au/

Wikipaedia: Fritz Hippler, NS-Filmemacher

Kirchheim am Neckar, protestant church, Kirchenbuch extract

Be Published